Native Fishes of Ohio

Native Fishes *of* Ohio

Daniel L. Rice
Gary Meszaros

THE KENT STATE UNIVERSITY PRESS
Kent, Ohio

© 2014 by The Kent State University Press, Kent, Ohio 44242
Photographs © 2014 by Gary Meszaros
All rights reserved
Library of Congress Catalog Number 2013043541
ISBN 978-1-60635-208-3
Manufactured in the United States of America

Library of Congress Cataloging-in-Publication Data

Rice, Daniel L.
  Native fishes of Ohio / Daniel L. Rice, Gary Meszaros.
      pages cm
  ISBN 978-1-60635-208-3 (pbk.) ∞
 1. Fishes—Ohio. 2. Fishes—Ohio—Identification.
 I. Meszaros, Gary. II. Title. III. Title: Fishes of Ohio.
  QL628.O3R53 2014
   597.09771—dc23
                                        2013043541

30 29 28 27 26   5 4 3

Contents

	Preface	vii
	Acknowledgments	xiii
1	Lampreys: Living Fossils	1
2	Paddlefish, Sturgeon, Gars, and More: Primitive and Unique Species	7
3	Minnows, Chubs, and Dace: Life in a Linear Environment	16
4	Shiners: Exploiting a Niche	31
5	Suckers: Swimming against the Current	44
6	Catfish: Night Stalkers	53
7	Sticklebacks, Mudminnows, Pirate Perch, and Others: Life in Small Places	60
8	Sunfish and Bass: Metallic Iridescence	69
9	Darters: A Rainbow of Colors	78
10	Fish of Lentic Habitats: Lake Erie	92
11	Aliens: Introduced Species	100
	Glossary	107
	Bibliography	109
	Index	111

Preface

The purpose of this book is to provide those people who are interested in natural history with a source of information about the amazing diversity of fishes that can be found in the rivers and streams of Ohio and to increase their awareness and appreciation of our aquatic heritage. Numbering more than 31,000 species, fish represent 50 percent of all living vertebrates. When studying these interesting creatures we can appreciate the marvelous complexity of how each species has adapted to fill its particular niche. Of the approximately 775 species of freshwater fishes found in North America, Milton B. Trautman recorded 166 species and 13 subspecies for the state in the 1981 revision of his classic work *The Fishes of Ohio*. Of this total, historical accounts and early collection data reveal that 18 species and one subspecies were not part of our native fauna. In more recent years, an additional six species have become established. These newcomers reached Ohio waters in a variety of ways. Some have entered the Great Lakes through the St. Lawrence River, and others have been purposely introduced for sport fishing. A few have arrived as stowaways in bilge water from oceangoing freighters; others, like the northern studfish, may have arrived from the dumping of bait buckets and/or aquariums. Our earliest introductions date back to the 1880s, with the stocking of various species of trout and salmon.

As terrestrial beings, it is hard to appreciate the complexities present in aquatic environments. This often leads to the belief that if there is water any given species of fish can live there. However, to reduce competition with other species, different species have evolved to fill the different habitats found in aquatic environments. These habitats are identified by characteristic features: type and size of a water body (lakes and streams), stream gradients, presence of riffles and pools, water clarity, substrate composition, and the presence or absence of aquatic vegetation and woody debris. Stream gradients are the driving force behind many habitat variables as current velocity determines a stream's ability to scour; erode; and transport silts, sands, gravels, and cobbles. The erosion and movement of these substrates in linear stream environments during high flows help determine the number and types of riffles present in a stream and are responsible for the formation of sand and gravel bars, pools, root wads, and undercut banks. It is this complex web of habitats that determines where a particular species can be found and allows for the diversity of species present in many streams.

A generalist can live in a wide array of habitats. Many fish, especially darters, are specialists, requiring specific water velocities and substrate compositions. Others require water of great clarity to survive. Siltation and pollution have greatly reduced populations of these specialized species. The changes in aquatic habitats over the last two hundred years have profoundly affected aquatic communities. Of the approximately 149 species and 9 subspecies documented as having been native to Ohio in the nineteenth century, the harelip sucker and blue pike are extinct. The Scioto madtom hasn't been collected since 1957, and most authorities consider it extinct. Eight species are now considered extirpated, twenty endangered, and twenty-two either threatened or listed as species of concern.

Surveys Past and Present

Ohio has a rich history of amateur and professional naturalists making observations of its flora and fauna. Between 1818 and 1820, C. S. Rafinesque, traveling by boat from Pittsburgh, Pennsylvania, to Louisville, Kentucky, made the first descriptions of fishes occurring in the Ohio River and associated tributary streams (Rafinesque 1820). His descriptions of the Ohio River unaltered by dams, with its corridors shrouded in deep forests, give modern readers insight into the early Ohio landscape. Jared P. Kirtland compiled the first lists of animals reported for the state as part of the *First Annual Report on the Geological Survey of the State of Ohio,* published in 1838. Included in this report were comments on the abundance, distribution, and biology for many species. Between 1838 and 1854, Kirtland published numerous articles in the *Boston Journal of Natural History* describing the fishes found in the Ohio River, Lake Erie, and their tributary streams. Among several important collections made in the last decade of the nineteenth century were James A. Henshall's in the Ohio River in 1888–89 and Philip H. Kirsh's in the Maumee River system in northwest Ohio in 1898. Kirsh's 1898 report is also important for the descriptions of his sampling stations along the Maumee and its tributaries. In 1901, while students at The Ohio State University, R. C. Osburn and E. B. Williamson used a horse and wagon to survey the fishes of Franklin County. Osburn published a list of Ohio fishes that same year, recording 134 native species and 3 introduced species.

Dr. Osburn and Edward L. Wickliff initiated the first statewide inventory of Ohio's native fishes in 1920, with funding provided by the state's Division of Fish and Game (now the Ohio Division of Wildlife). Milton Trautman first started collecting with Osburn and Wickliff in 1925, and in 1930 they published a revised fish list for the state. Trautman continued these surveys for another twenty-five years, leading to his classic work, *The Fishes of Ohio,* published in 1957. Working with students, Trautman continued to do surveys in central Ohio, particularly Big Darby Creek. A revised edition of Trautman's book was released in 1981. Ted Cavender, replacing Trautman as the curator of fishes at the Ohio State University Museum of Biological Diversity, continued the museum's tradition of fish surveys in central Ohio. In the late 1970s, the Ohio Environmental Protection Agency (OEPA), as part of its efforts to implement the Clean Water Act and set pollution standards, developed criteria based on fish and aquatic macroinvertebrate communities. Starting in 1979, OEPA instituted systematic fish surveys using electro-fishing gear. The Ohio Department of Transportation also conducted fish surveys as part of its environmental assessment for bridge and road projects. In 1981, the junior author, Dan Rice, a biologist with the Ohio Department of Natural Resources (ODNR), began surveys collecting data on rare and endangered fish species. Many exciting discoveries were made over the next twenty years. Today surveys by OEPA, ODNR, and others continue adding to our knowledge of Ohio's fish; particularly noteworthy has been the recent fieldwork conducted by Brian Zimmerman and Justin Baker of the OSU Museum with funding from the Ohio Division of Wildlife.

The addition of electro-fishing gear in the sampling of fish populations has also brought much new data on the status and distribution of many of Ohio's large river species. Earlier information often came from either commercial fishermen or the different types of trap nets employed by the Ohio Division of Wildlife. While effective, these nets required significant time and labor, which limited their use in general surveys on large rivers and lakes. In addition to the advancement of electro-fishing as a sampling tool, the recent use of smaller trawl nets to sample the deeper pools of the state's larger rivers has added important new data on the species inhabiting these hard-to-reach habitats. The culmination of all this work has been a clearer picture of the distribution, abundance, and status of Ohio's fish species.

A Changed Environment

Since the first European settlement of Ohio, people have been changing the rivers, streams, and lakes to suit their needs. These changes invariably resulted in diminished habitat and water quality for resident aquatic communities. Mill dams, which the first pioneers erected on the smaller streams, blocked spawning runs; these were followed by larger dams, used for flood control and recreation. While the smaller mill and low head dams might allow for passage of some fish during high water flows, the larger dams blocked all upstream and downstream movement. The pools these dams formed also acted as basins for silt deposition, smothering sand, gravel, and cobble substrates, which eliminated or greatly reduced clear water species. Today, the Ohio River has a system of high lift locks and dams, which creates a continuous series of deep pools. Clearing of the state's original forest also destabilized stream banks, which led to increased erosion and channel cutting. The growth of cities and use of fertilizers on crop land have increased the amount of nitrogen and phosphorus runoff, which has the undesirable side effect of fueling green algae and phytoplankton growth.

Perhaps no water body better illustrates the effects of pollution than Lake Erie. Throughout the last century the lake has undergone many changes. Early observers recorded a clean lake with many valuable fish, like blue pike, lake sturgeon, whitefish, and cisco. By 1960, overfishing and pollution from metropolitan areas had eliminated or greatly reduced these species. By the 1970s, many biologists had declared Lake Erie dead. Pollution had contributed to large growths of plankton, which caused populations of less desirable species, like gizzard shad, to proliferate to the detriment of other species. The 1980s saw the accidental introduction of zebra mussels, followed by the round goby, a predatory fish species released from ship ballast, in the 1990s. Ironically, the zebra mussels cleared the lake's waters by filtering out algae and other suspended particles, but they had a negative effect on the thriving walleye population. With the twenty-first century come new problems. Warmer waters and ever increasing amounts of phosphorus runoff from agricultural lands have created large blooms of toxic algae. Seasonal dead zones are further evidence of a fundamental imbalance in the lake's ecosystem.

Stream surveys conducted since the 1980s point to improved water quality. This is due partly to the Clean Water Act helping control both point and nonpoint pollution. Many of Ohio's larger municipalities have also upgraded sewage treatment. Industrial discharge has been reduced and in some cases eliminated. Reclamation from strip-mining activities in eastern Ohio has reduced acid wastes affecting streams in that region. The Scioto River south of Columbus is a notable example of this improving water quality; habitat-sensitive species like the Tippecanoe darter, once restricted to tributaries such as Deer Creek and Big Darby Creek, are now found in the lower and middle Scioto River as far upstream as Columbus. A renewed emphasis on protection and restoration of riparian corridors, particularly on Ohio's designated scenic rivers, has helped reduce stream bank erosion. Fish previously considered uncommon are now being caught in increasing numbers, and gradual range extensions have been observed for others.

Native Fishes of Ohio deals with those species that originally inhabited the state or have arrived there since the early nineteenth century. Throughout the book, species are not presented in phylogenetic order but instead are distributed relatively evenly throughout various chapters. In almost all cases, at least one living image, which Gary Meszaros photographed over many years, is provided. During his career with the Ohio Department of Natural Resources, Dan Rice collected voucher specimens of rare species Gary used in some of the photos; these are held at the Ohio State Museum of Comparative Zoology and the Cleveland Museum of Natural History.

Acknowledgments

Many people have contributed their time and expertise to this project. Gary Meszaros would like to thank Tim Matson of the Cleveland Museum of Natural History for introducing him to the fishes of northeast Ohio. Dan Rice spent many memorable hours with George Phinney of Otterbein College sampling glacial lakes and pursuing Ohio's rarest stream species. Mark Barnes of the Center for Lake Erie Area Research and Ted Cavender of the Ohio State University Museum of Biological Diversity were also instrumental in honing Dan Rice's fish identification skills and spent many enjoyable hours with him in Ohio's rivers and streams.

Many individuals, both amateur and professional, have assisted the authors in their pursuit of fish or by providing valuable information about various species. Especially helpful as seining partners, in addition to those mentioned above, were Bob Gable, Jim McCormac, Mike Hoggarth, Stu Lewis, Jeff Riebe, Al Staffan, Ed Stroh, and Tom Watters. A number of student interns from Otterbein College assisted in stream surveys: Megan Devito, Brook McDonald, Tara Chin, Jason Ferguson, Jim Gates, Megan Michaels, Diana Lee, Scott Ross, and Stacy Xenakis. The fishery biologists associated with OEPA's Surface Water Section were also generous with their time, equipment, and expertise; Brian Alsdorf, Dennis Mishne, Ed Rankin, Randy Sanders, Marc Smith, Roger Thoma, and Chris Yoder were especially helpful.

Fishery biologists within the Ohio Division of Wildlife have also helped to make this book a better one—especially Daryl Allison, Phil Hillman, Ken Paxton, Dave Ross, and Doug Sweet. Many naturalists and fish enthusiasts have generously donated their time or expertise, among them Mac Albin, Jim Bissell, Craig Ciola, Todd Crail, Guy Denny, Marc Kibbey, Jane Meszaros, Carolyn Platt, Ralph Pfingsten, John Pogacnik, Andy White, Jeff Wolfinger, and Brian Zimmerman.

We would especially like to thank Tim Matson of the Cleveland Museum of Natural History and Brian Zimmerman of the Ohio State University

Museum of Biological Diversity, Fish Division for their critical reviews of this manuscript. The project benefitted from their knowledge of Ohio fishes and many editorial suggestions.

Finally, we would also like to thank Will Underwood, the rest of The Kent State University Press staff, and copyeditor Erin Holman for their support in making this publication possible.

Lampreys
Living Fossils

CHAPTER 1

The first primitive vertebrates that swam in our oceans were jawless fishes. Over millions of years, fish with movable jaws began to appear. This evolutionary advancement enabled these early species to capture and hold prey. Today, all that remains of the jawless fish are the hagfishes and lampreys, the latter sometimes referred to as living fossils The few fossil remains that have been found (lamprey bodies are composed of soft tissue) indicate that they have survived unchanged since the Devonian period, 360 million years ago. During their long existence, they have survived at least four major extinction events affecting life on this planet, including the one some 65 million years ago that wiped out the dinosaurs. Lampreys are one of nature's evolutionary success stories.

Lampreys are readily identified by their smooth, eellike bodies, seven gill openings, and oral discs, or suckers, which surround their mouths. Their cartilaginous skeletons lack the pelvic and pectoral fins characteristic of bony fish. All lampreys have an extended juvenile stage in which the larva, or ammocoetes, lack functioning eyes and expanded oral disc. Adults of some species parasitize other fish. They use their oral discs to firmly attach themselves to a host and their rasping tongues in combination with the oral disc's sharp teeth to create a wound through which to ingest blood and other body fluids. Not all lampreys are parasitic; there are also nonparasitic lampreys, which represent degenerative forms of parasitic species. Identification of the various species is based on a combination of the oral disc and associated teeth, pigmentation patterns, and characteristics of dorsal fins. Teeth are not as well developed in nonparasitic lampreys but are nonetheless important in species identification.

There are ten worldwide genera of lampreys, comprising about forty species. Restricted primarily to temperate waters, they inhabit both freshwater and marine environments. Ohio's seven species are divided among four genera; the *Icthyomyzon, Lampetra, Lethenteron,* and *Petromyzon*. Three of these—silver, Ohio, and sea lamprey—are parasitic. The remaining four brook lampreys are nonparasitic: least brook, northern brook, mountain brook, and American brook lampreys. Adult nonparasitic lampreys are considerably smaller than their parasitic counterparts, averaging about seven inches in length. In comparison, spawning silver and Ohio lampreys can reach fourteen inches. Nonnative sea lampreys are by far the largest, reaching a length of two feet or more.

All lampreys spawn in similar fashion. In spring, sexually mature adults move onto gravel riffles in rivers and streams. A male excavates a shallow nest at the head of a riffle, using its oral disc to move gravel, and a female initiates spawning by moving onto the nest. The male and female will vibrate against each other, releasing milt (sperm) and eggs into the nest. One pair will initiate spawning with other pairs joining in. Where ranges overlap, different species may utilize the same nests. In a Pennsylvania study, mountain brook lampreys were observed sharing the same nests with Ohio lampreys (Cooper 1983). During the height of spawning activity, the adults seem oblivious to their surroundings and can be easily observed.

Breeding takes place in the spring and is correlated with water temperature. When temperatures exceed fifty degrees Fahrenheit, males begin to move onto riffles to excavate nests and await females. Parasitic females produce more eggs than the smaller, nonparasitic females: more than twenty thousand, compared to fewer than two thousand in a study by M. W. Hardisty (1963). Least brook lampreys in southern Ohio streams tend to be the first to initiate spawning; their spawning activities are typically reported in late March and early April. Other species spawn later in the spring, with peak activity often reported for late April and early May. In northern Ohio, northern and mountain brook lampreys have been observed spawning during the first week of May.

Larval stages are similar for all lampreys. A fertilized egg hatches into a larva, referred to as an ammocoete. Newly hatched ammocoetes drift into downstream pools and eddies, where they burrow into clean substrates composed of organic debris, in which they will spend the next four to seven years, protected from predators. At this point, they are blind and their oral discs and associated teeth are not fully developed. Efficient feeders, they produce strands of mucus that trap passing food particles. However, they are easily suffocated by depositions of heavy silts, particularly those containing clay. Transformation from ammocoete to adult occurs in the fall; thus, newly transformed individuals overwinter as adults. Transformation involves opening of the eyes, expansion of the oral disc, and final formation of the circumoral teeth surrounding the mouth. In the case of the nonparasitic species, transformation also involves the closing of the alimentary tract and development of the reproductive organs.

At this point in the lampreys' life cycle, parasitic and nonparasitic species diverge. Nonparasitic adults move onto suitable riffles in the spring, spawn, and die, leaving their fertilized eggs to carry on the next generation. Newly transformed adults of parasitic species also overwinter in streams where they were spawned, but, unlike nonparasitic species, their alimentary tracts do not close off and they do not become sexually mature. The following spring, they drift downstream into deep pools, searching for suitable hosts. Once attached to a host fish, where it will remain for one or two years, the lamprey acts as an external parasite. During this stage, the parasitic lampreys finally reach sexual maturity. In spring, sexually mature adults migrate upstream into tributaries where they construct their nests on suitable riffles prior to spawning. Following spawning, the fate of all lampreys is the same. Post-spawning adults, their energies spent in reproduction and unable to eat, drift into pools and eddies to die.

Populations of Ohio lampreys are restricted to the Ohio River and its tributaries. The authors collected spawning adults in the Little Muskingum River in Washington County in 2001, and there is a 2012 collection from Yellow Creek in Jefferson County. Other small, undocumented populations may still exist in other Ohio River tributaries. Records of spawning silver lampreys were found in both Lake Erie and Ohio River drainages. In the mid-nineteenth century, Kirtland (1851) reported this species as abundant in Lake Erie with large numbers of spawning adults in streams around Cleveland. Numbers reported by commercial fishermen on the lake fell dramatically after the turn of the twentieth century, and by 1951 not a single lamprey was observed in the commercial catch (Trautman 1981). Until Brian Zimmerman discovered spawning adults in Conneaut Creek in 2013, the only recent records of silver lampreys in the Lake Erie drainage had been in 1972, from the lower Chagrin River (personal communication). A small population is known in Leading Creek in Meigs County, part of the Ohio River drainage, and since the late 1980s, there have been sporadic records of adults from the lower Scioto River and some of its tributaries like Salt Creek in Vinton County. In 2013, Brian Zimmerman also identified spawning adults in the Shade and Little Scioto Rivers in southern Ohio (personal communication).

Endangered mountain and northern brook lampreys have the most restricted ranges in Ohio. There are 2012 records for spawning mountain brook lampreys in the lower Kokosing River in Knox County. In the Mahoning system, there are 2012 records for both the South Fork of Eagle Creek and the West Branch of the Mahoning River upstream of West Branch Reservoir in Portage County. Populations of northern brook lampreys are still known for headwater tributaries of the Grand and Ashtabula Rivers as well as Conneaut Creek in northeast Ohio. There are old records for this species from the lower Scioto drainage in central and southern Ohio, but none had been reported from this area in recent years until 2013 when Brian Zimmerman captured spawning adults in the Little Scioto River, an Ohio River tributary in Jackson and Scioto Counties (personal communication). American brook lampreys can still be found in some of the high gradient streams throughout the state, including the Chagrin River system in northeast Ohio, the St. Joseph system in northwest Ohio, and the Killbuck Creek system in Wayne and Holmes Counties. The largest populations may be those found in the Mad River system in Champaign and Logan Counties. Least brook lampreys are the smallest and most common of our species. These inhabit small high gradient streams throughout unglaciated Ohio.

Non-parasitic least brook lampreys are the smallest and most widely distributed of Ohio's seven species. They can be found spawning in late March and early April in small, high-gradient streams in southeastern Ohio.

The pattern of the circumoral teeth on parasitic Ohio lampreys distinguishes them from similar silver lampreys. The species is endangered in Ohio; its spawning adults are known from the Little Muskingum River in Muskingum County and Yellow Creek in Jefferson County.

Endangered mountain brook lampreys are restricted to a few high-quality streams like the Kokosing River in Knox County and the West Branch of the Mahoning River, especially the South Fork of Eagle Creek in Portage County.

Endangered northern brook lampreys spawn in clear headwater tributaries of the Grand and Ashtabula Rivers. Another population has recently been documented in the Little Scioto River, an Ohio River tributary in southern Ohio.

Pharyngeal slits on this Ohio lamprey mark the position of its gills. Water entering the mouth passes over the gills before exiting through these openings.

Paddlefish, Sturgeon, Gars, and More
Primitive and Unique Species

CHAPTER 2

Within Ohio waters swim relict fish that were present when Tyrannosaurus rex was making life undesirable for other terrestrial forms of life. Indeed, they have changed little from their predecessors and are sometimes referred to as living fossils. Included in this group are the sturgeon, paddlefish, and gars, which represent some of North America's largest freshwater fish. Other primitive though slightly more advanced species include the mooneyes and goldeyes in the Family Hiodontidae, the bowfin, and members of the herring family, like shad and skipjack herring.

As the only extant members of Polyodontidae, paddlefish represent one of our oldest species. Fossil evidence of this unique fish predates the rise of the dinosaurs by 50 million years. Paddlefish are instantly recognized by their extremely large mouths and long paddle-shaped snouts, which can be a third of their overall length. Were it not for its head, the paddlefish would resemble a shark in form and coloration. Slate gray, it is covered by smooth skin and has a sharklike tail and a skeleton composed primarily of cartilage. These primitive fish are highly specialized filter feeders with gill rakers that can filter zooplankton and other small crustaceans from water. It was once thought that this species used its paddle-shaped snout to probe for invertebrates. Recent research has determined that a number of electrosensory receptors in the fish's snout are used to detect weak electrical fields given off by zooplankton.

Residents of the larger river systems of the Mississippi drainage, paddlefish frequent areas of slow current, especially oxbows and backwaters.

Spawning occurs in spring, during periods of high flow on gravel bars. Adhesive eggs hatch in approximately seven days, with young drifting downstream into quiet pools.

Paddlefish can reach five feet in length and weigh up to eighty pounds. Females of this long-lived species do not reach sexual maturity until their ninth or tenth year, and some individuals live fifty years. Before 1900, paddlefish were common in the Ohio and Scioto Rivers; steep declines in their numbers were noted after the construction of the first dams. Today they are found in small numbers in the Ohio River downstream from Portsmouth. Nineteenth-century records show that a small population also existed in Lake Erie. Recently the species' eggs have been targeted as a source of caviar. With the collapse of the Caspian sturgeon population, which formerly accounted for a large share of the world's caviar, the market's interest has focused on dwindling paddlefish populations in the upper Mississippi River.

Like the paddlefish, the shovelnose sturgeon has a broad, flattened, spade-shaped snout. Its mouth is located on its ventral surface, with a row of four barbels placed between the mouth and snout. Rather than scales, this fish is covered by a series of bony plates and a long whiplike filament extending from the upper lobe of the caudal fin. The smaller of the two species, it seldom exceeds five pounds. Native to large rivers of the Mississippi and Missouri River systems this sturgeon frequents areas of moderate to swift current. A highly protrusible mouth is used to pick up a variety of macroinvertebrates and small fish. Spawning occurs in spring over gravel substrates in swift current. Females reach sexual maturity in their sixth or seventh year, with spawning occurring every few years thereafter. Recent studies indicate a maximum life span of twelve years for populations in the lower Mississippi River (Morrow et al. 1998).

Shovelnose sturgeon were once abundant in the Ohio River as far upstream as Marietta in Washington County. There are no historic records or reports, however, from the lower sections of some of our larger streams. The populations began to decline following the early construction of navigation dams, and by 1950 only an occasional specimen was reported above Portsmouth. A small population of this endangered species still survives between Portsmouth and the Indiana line. In 2002, the Division of Wildlife initiated a five-year effort to reintroduce shovelnose sturgeon into the lower Scioto River. Tagged adults are occasionally reported, but to date there has been no evidence of successful reproduction.

The lake sturgeon is equipped with five rows of bony plates, or scutes, and a torpedo-shaped body with a shark-like tail. It uses its spadelike snout to stir up bottom substrates in search of macroinvertebrates and four sensory barbels anterior of the mouth to locate prey, which it then sucks off the bottom with its protrusible lips. Unlike shovelnose sturgeon, which favors areas of moderate to swift current in large rivers, lake sturgeon are denizens of large lakes in the eastern half of the United States and Canada. This state endangered species was historically abundant in both Lake Erie and the Ohio River. One of Ohio's largest freshwater species, it can weigh over one hundred pounds and reach five feet in length. Long-lived, females do not reach sexual maturity until their twentieth year. While large females are capable of producing prodigious quantities of eggs, they do so only every three to four years.

At the beginning of the twentieth century, lake sturgeon were commercially exploited for both their eggs and flesh and as a source of isinglass, a clarifying agent used in jellies, glues, and glass. Prior to European settlement, many rivers, such as the Maumee, Cuyahoga, and Scioto, were important spring spawning sites for lake sturgeon. Today the American Fisheries Society has listed this species as threatened in every state throughout its range. A combination of delayed reproduction and loss of spawning habitat has made it hard for this species to rebound even when protected.

Gars are an ancient order with ties to the Cretaceous period. Seven surviving species are all that remain of this primitive group; five are restricted to North America, and the other two are found in South America and Cuba. Gars are easily identified by their elongate, cylindrical bodies and narrow jaws filled with needlelike teeth. Many species are characterized by the spots on their fins and dorsal surfaces, although these patterns are too variable to be used in identifying individual species. All gars are armored in a tough skin covered by a series of hard ganoid scales, which Native Americans sometimes used as spear points. Gars are one of a few fish possessing vascularized swim bladders, which they can supply with oxygen by gulping air from the surface. This adaptation allows them to tolerate habitat conditions that would kill most other fish. Gars are voracious predators, feeding primarily on small fish. Where abundant, they can be a bane to many fishermen, stripping bait from hooks with impunity.

Three of the seven gar species—the longnose, shortnose, and spotted—are residents of Ohio. A fourth species, the alligator gar, native to the rivers of the southern United States is known from a few Ohio River records. Longnose gars are Ohio's most common species. Although still abundant in suitable habitats in both Lake Erie and Ohio River drainages, their numbers have declined since the early twentieth century. Gars prefer calm waters with aquatic vegetation. In Lake Erie, longnose gars are often found in harbors and backwaters, with spawning occurring in streams on shallow riffles. Their large sticky green eggs are poisonous to humans. In Lake Erie, spawning occurs wherever beds of aquatic vegetation can be found. Old females can reach lengths of fifty-five inches, although males seldom exceed thirty-six inches.

Shortnose gars are identified by their shorter snouts. On them, the spotted pattern is much reduced, being largely confined to the posterior fins and body. Widespread in the Mississippi River system, they inhabit large rivers, backwaters, and oxbows. This species is largely restricted to the Ohio River and a few of its tributaries; the majority of our records were taken from overflow ponds adjacent to the Scioto River between 1939 and 1950. During stream surveys conducted between 1979 and 1995, only eleven individuals of this endangered species were captured (Sanders et al. 1999). Spawning activities and growth of young are dependent on backwater habitats where the adhesive eggs are scattered over submerged vegetation.

Spotted gars, as the name implies, are characterized by the profusion of dark spots that cover their fins and body, including head and jaws. A short, broad snout covered in spots differentiates the spotted gar from the more common longnose gar. Ohio's population of this southern species has always been restricted to Lake Erie, the northern limit of its range. These were originally found in clear water embayments with beds of aquatic vegetation. As turbidity levels in the lake increased and beds of submerged aquatics dwindled, Ohio's population gradually declined. In recent years, there have been few reports of spotted gars, now listed as endangered in Ohio.

Like the gars, to whom it is most closely related, the bowfin is the sole survivor of another primitive order, the Amiiformes, which flourished during the Jurassic and Cretaceous periods. No other fish looks quite like a bowfin. Green in color with a stout somewhat elongated body, it has an elongated dorsal fin and a black spot at the upper edge of its caudal fin. Slightly more advanced than gars and sturgeon, bowfin are covered by true scales characteristic of more modern fish, but they still retain significant amounts of cartilage in their skeletons. Like gars, they also have modified air bladders, which allow them to breath surface air. They have been reported to survive droughts by burrowing into mud, much like African lungfish. Females can reach lengths of thirty-six inches, and weights over twenty pounds have been reported for the species. Males are smaller, seldom exceeding twenty-four inches.

Bowfin inhabit both lakes and streams with clear water and abundant growths of aquatic vegetation. Like gars, they frequent oxbows, sloughs, and backwaters and are especially common in the marshes of the western basin of Lake Erie. Bowfin are aggressive predators, eating a variety of fish, crayfish, insects, amphibians, and anything else of suitable size. In spring, male bowfin build nests usually composed of bits of vegetation. After a female deposits her eggs, the male aggressively guards the nest until the young hatch. Recently hatched fry form a ball and follow the male around for several weeks before dispersing. No other North American fish protects its young for as long a period.

Mooneyes and goldeyes represent the only survivors of the Family Hiodontidae. Slab-sided fish with small heads, large eyes, and forked tails, they resemble shad or herrings. Prominent tooth patches found on both the tongue and roof of the mouth help hold prey. Mooneyes get their name from their silvery eyes, while a gold body gives the goldeye its name. They are typically twelve inches long. Both species are opportunistic feeders, preying on a large variety of macroinvertebrates, terrestrial insects, and small fish.

Goldeyes have always been restricted to the Ohio River and some of its larger tributaries, and mooneyes are found in both the Lake Erie and Ohio River drainages. After the turn of the twentieth century, increasing turbidity and silt loads found in the state's rivers and streams favored the goldeye, while mooneyes, which depended on clearer waters, began to decline. Improvements in water quality since the late 1980s have once again favored the mooneyes, which currently outnumber the goldeyes. Very few goldeyes have been found in recent years, and the species is now listed as endangered.

The Clupeidae is another ancient group of fishes. This large family, more than two hundred species worldwide, is represented in North America by eleven species in three genera. Only three of these, skipjack herring and gizzard and threadfin shad, are native to Ohio waters. Members of this family tend to be laterally compressed, with deep bodies, large eyes, and forked tails. They have single soft-rayed dorsal fins and are covered by large silvery scales, which are easily peeled off. Gizzard shad and other members of the genus *Dorosoma* are distinguished from skipjack herring, in the genus *Alosa* by a greatly elongated last ray on the dorsal fin, especially on the threadfin shad. As with other members of the family, both shad and skipjack herring form large schools when feeding. During spawning, the adhesive eggs are scattered over a variety of substrates, with no parental care.

Widespread throughout the Mississippi Basin, skipjack herring in Ohio have always been restricted to the Ohio River and some of its larger tributaries, while threadfin shad are known only from a few recent records. Skipjack herring are often found in areas with fast current and low turbidity, where they feed primarily on shiners and other small fish. Spawning is thought to occur over sand and gravel swept by strong current. Adults typically reach lengths of fourteen inches.

The wide-ranging gizzard shad occupy much of the eastern United States. They are abundant in both Lake Erie and the Ohio River. Thriving in turbid water, gizzard shad are vegetarians, using their small subterminal mouths to graze on beds of algae or other detritus and also use their gill rakers to filter phytoplankton. The gizzard shad is sensitive to sudden changes in water temperature, and massive die-offs are sometimes observed along the Lake Erie shoreline. Adults are often fifteen inches long. Unlike the skipjack herring, gizzard shad are undesirable as a human food source.

American eels are the sole North American representatives of the Family Anguillidae, which worldwide comprises nineteen species, including the closely related European eel. Although not as primitive as gars and sturgeon, eels are certainly unique among freshwater fish in both their life cycle and physical appearance. Eels are readily identified by their long, snakelike bodies and small eyes. Though armed with numerous small teeth, they have weak jaws and must consume their prey whole or by tearing it apart, employing a spinning motion. Small scales and a layer of slime make them difficult to handle. Adult eels are typically olive green. Long dorsal and anal fins fuse with the rounded caudal fin to form a fringe on the posterior half of their bodies. Capable of breathing through their skins, they have been known to travel overland to reach new sources of water.

All of the Anguillidae have similar life histories, which are among the most complex of any family. American eels spend most of their lives in fresh and saltwater habitats along the Atlantic and Gulf Coasts. Sexually mature adults migrate to the North Atlantic, where they spawn and die. Larval eels drift with the ocean current for up to a year before making their way back to coastal waters. American eels have two juvenile stages. In the first they lack pigment and are called glass eels. In the second, or elver, stage the young eels slowly develop into sexually immature adults, often referred to as yellow eels. It is at this stage that young eels migrate into freshwater habitats. A secretive species, the eel hides under rocks and logs, only coming out at night to prey on a variety of dead and live animal matter. Females grow larger than males, typically reaching three feet.

In the past, eels were not uncommon in the Ohio River drainage. It is thought that the completion of the Welland Canal in 1829 provided their first access into the Great Lakes drainage. During the latter part of the twentieth century, the Ohio Fish Commission released thousands of elvers throughout the state in an effort to augment populations. While a few individuals of this threatened species are occasionally caught, the extensive network of dams on many of our tributary streams has blocked access to much of their former habitat.

American eels are Ohio's only fish that spend their lives in fresh water and eventually return to the sea to breed.

The postopercular spot, large eyes, and elongated dorsal ray are good field marks for gizzard shad. Important prey items for a variety of sportfish, they are abundant in Lake Erie and large rivers throughout Ohio.

Eels are identified by their smooth, snakelike bodies, lack of pelvic fins, and long dorsal and anal fins fused with the tail. They spawn in salt water, and young eels, called elvers, ascend freshwater tributaries to mature.

The skipjack herring can be identified by its protruding lower jaw; forked tail; and short, concave dorsal fin. These fish are common in the Ohio River.

Ohio's most common species, the longnose gar, is found throughout Ohio. These fish are sometimes observed floating near the surface in aquatic vegetation.

The bowfin is easily identified by its greenish color, long dorsal fin, and black tail spot. It is especially common in the vegetated wetlands and marshes of northeastern Ohio.

The elongated snouts of longnose gars serve to distinguish them from shortnose and spotted gars. These fish feed primarily on small fish: their needle-sharp teeth are effective in capturing and holding prey.

Minnows, Chubs, and Dace
Life in a Linear Environment

CHAPTER 3

Cyprinids make up the largest family of freshwater fish in the world with more than two thousand species grouped into more than two hundred genera. North America is home to about three hundred species and fifty genera. They are distinguished by the absence of a stomach, lack of teeth, and the presence of a swim bladder. Many have pharyngeal teeth, formed from modifications to the last (fifth) set of gill rakers. This enables them to crush harder food items, especially snails, bivalves, and small crustaceans. These teeth are species specific, with the size and shape reflecting their various diets. Cyprinids have single dorsal fins with nine or fewer rays, pelvic fins positioned abdominally, and pectoral fins set low on their sides. With few exceptions, they lack spines on their dorsal and anal rays; thus the fins are soft and flexible. Members of the minnow family have excellent hearing; a series of small bones, the Weberian ossicles, helps minnows detect potential predators. They can also release pheromones to warn others of possible danger.

Cyprinids are well represented in the western United States. Members of the family include many endemic species, including one of the largest, the Colorado pikeminnow. This monster can attain lengths of six feet and weigh over one hundred pounds. Most cyprinids are far smaller, however, often averaging less than four inches. They frequently congregate in large schools while feeding and spawning. Minnows play an important role in aquatic ecosystems; they are a major prey item for larger fish in the food chain. Emerald and spottail shiners are harvested commercially in Lake Erie for use as live bait, while fathead minnows and golden shiners are raised through aquaculture to supply inland markets. Ohio cyprinids are often divided into four groups: minnows, chubs, dace, and shiners (discussed in chapter 4). All are principally stream species that have evolved to exploit these linear habitats. Differences in feeding and reproduction reflect these adaptations.

Minnows

Six genera bear the name minnow: *Campostoma, Exoglossum, Hybognathus, Opsopoeodus, Phenacobius,* and *Pimephales*. These encompass more than twenty species in North America, of which eight are found in Ohio. One other species, the silverjaw minnow, is actually a shiner and is discussed in the next chapter. Mississippi silvery minnows of the genus *Hybognathus* were first known in Ohio from pre-1900 collections made in tributaries of the Ohio River. They were not recorded again until 1981, when a single specimen was captured in the Great Miami River. This southern species is common in lowland streams of the Mississippi drainage. Threatened tongue-tied minnows of the genus *Exoglossum* are now largely restricted to the Mad River drainage in Champaign County. Endangered pugnose minnows (*Opsopoeodus*) have been reduced to a few glacial lakes in northern Ohio and the St. Marys River in Mercer County. Found in lentic habitats with clear water and beds of submerged vegetation, they quickly disappeared from Lake Erie and the larger streams during the twentieth century as habitat conditions deteriorated. The five remaining species are all common and widespread. One of Ohio's most abundant species, bluntnose minnows (*Pimephales*) are pool dwellers found in streams of all sizes. Closely related bullhead minnows are normally restricted to the state's largest rivers. The third member of this genus, the fathead minnow, is one of Ohio's most pollution-tolerant species, preferring lentic habitats and turbid waters. Free from competition, the fathead reaches its greatest abundance in these situations. These minnows are commonly sold as bait and have been released into many streams as bait-bucket introductions. Stoneroller minnows (*Campostoma*) are one of Ohio's most abundant fish. They are associated with the riffles and runs of the larger streams and generally avoid small headwaters. They are the state's largest minnow, attaining lengths of seven inches. Suckermouth minnows (*Phenacobius*) are a prairie stream species that invaded the western half of Ohio as original forests were cleared. Inhabitants of riffles, they have adapted to the turbid water of larger streams and are now found as far east as the Muskingum River and its tributaries.

Breeding minnows lack the bright colors seen in darters, although some, like the fathead and bluntnose, are flushed with rose. The heads of bluntnose, bullhead, and fathead minnows swell and darken during the breeding season. These minnows also develop prominent nodes or tubercles on their faces and bodies. Prominently marked with orange, yellow, black, and tan, breeding male stonerollers are one of Ohio's most colorful species. Their heads and bodies are also covered with large white tubercles.

Pugnose, bluntnose, fathead, and bullhead minnows are all cavity spawners. Males excavate and defend cavities underneath rocks, logs, or other objects. Multiple females may lay eggs in the same nest, with males remaining to guard and aerate the eggs. Eggs are usually attached to the undersides of these cavities. Stonerollers, like other minnow species, generally utilize nests constructed by chubs. Tongue-tied minnows construct raised mounds from gravel, transported by the male. Fertilized eggs fall over gravel substrates, with both sexes departing the nest.

Among the minnows, stonerollers are grazers, feeding on beds of filamentous green algae. Their common name, rot-gut minnow, refers to their long, black alimentary tract, necessary for the breakdown of cellulose found in plant material. Stonerollers will also eat a variety of other plants and animals, including aquatic insects and microcrustacea, which they glean from the surface of rocks and stones. Tongue-tied minnows are specialists, feeding on insect larvae and small crustaceans they pick from the stream bottom. Bluntnose minnows feed almost exclusively on zooplankton; they can become abundant in ponded streams and river oxbows. Fathead and bullhead minnows are omnivorous, consuming organic material as well as small aquatic insects. Pugnose minnows, with their small, upturned mouths, pick insect larva and other food from the water's surface.

Several species show a remarkable tolerance for polluted and degraded water. Stoneroller populations can rise dramatically in streams where nitrates and phosphorus runoff result in rampant green algae growths. Bluntnose and bullhead minnows also seem unaffected by turbid water and organic enrichment. Their gills eliminate carbon dioxide, ammonia, and other waste while taking in oxygen. Fathead minnows are perhaps the most tolerant, surviving exposure to organic and chemical pollutants lethal to most species. For this reason, fatheads are the animal of choice when determining toxicity levels in our rivers and streams. Suckermouth minnows also thrive in water rich in organic material, provided riffles and runs are swept clean.

Chubs

Chubs are a group of fishes adapted almost exclusively to riverine systems. There are a large number of endemic species found in the southern regions of the United States. The taxonomy of many of our eastern chubs is currently undergoing major revisions based on the results of molecular and DNA studies. Eight species are currently found in Ohio, split among five genera: *Macrhybopsis, Hybopsis, Erimystax, Nocomis,* and *Semotilus*. With the exception of the silver chub (*Macrhybopsis*), found in both Lake Erie and the Ohio River, they are riverine. In Lake Erie, silver chubs have been reported from waters as deep as sixty feet. Shoal chubs, in the same genus, inhabit the large rivers, like the Ohio, where they feed over sand and gravel. There are historic records from the lower Muskingum River, but none have been taken there in over sixty years. In 2012, Brian Zimmerman captured a small number in the Ohio and Great Miami Rivers (personal communication). Hard-to-catch gravel and streamline chubs are both members of the genus *Erimystax,* whose members are gold with rounded bodies and large eyes. Small populations of streamline chubs were, until recently, found primarily in the Kokosing, Walhonding, and Big Darby Rivers. Inhabitants of riffles and runs, their numbers have been growing in recent years due to improved water qualities. They are now found throughout the middle and lower Scioto and upper Muskingum basins and have even invaded the upper Ohio River main stem. Gravel chubs frequent similar habitats and reach their greatest abundance in large rivers, like the Scioto, Muskingum, and Great and Little Miami.

River and hornyhead chubs are closely related members of the genus *Nocomis*. Both formerly had wide distributions in Lake Erie and Ohio River drainages. River chubs, as their name implies, favor larger streams. They are one of Ohio's largest native cyprinids, approaching almost twelve inches in length. Hornyhead chubs, named for the males' breeding tubercles, favor more moderate-sized streams. Unlike river chubs, hornyheads are restricted to streams in the glaciated portion of Ohio. In rivers where populations overlap, like the upper Cuyahoga and Kokosing, hornyheads are common in the upper reaches, while river chubs frequent the lower reaches. Pollution and siltation have eliminated some populations and the distribution and abundance of both species are now greatly reduced. Bigeye chubs (*Hybopsis*) are intolerant of turbid water. In the last half of the twentieth century, they were found in many streams throughout the state. Pollution and increasing water turbidity led to a widespread loss of many of these populations. Today the Kokosing and Walhonding Rivers remain one of their strongholds, and the species has recently (since the turn of the twenty-first century) expanded into the upper Muskingum and Tuscarawas Rivers. Bigeye populations have also been increasing in the Scioto and Great Miami basins. The creek chub (*Semotilus*) is one of the state's most common and widespread species, reaching its greatest abundance in smaller tributaries. Like the river chub, they can reach lengths of twelve inches and are frequently caught by trout fisherman.

Nest-building habits of spawning river and hornyhead chubs have been extensively documented. Males excavate pits in areas where moderate to swift currents flow over gravel substrates. These circular pits may be up to fifteen inches in diameter and six inches deep. Once the females appear, the males then fill in these pits creating a dome-shaped mound of gravel seven to eight inches in height. Males of both species guard their nests from other males. Creek chubs also excavate pits. Both *Nocomis* and *Semotilus* are known for the large tubercles displayed on the heads of breeding males. Breeding male hornyhead and river chubs develop swollen heads, which are useful for moving stones and gravel. Silver and shoal chubs in the genus *Macrhybopsis* are broadcast spawners: eggs released during their spawning fall to the bottom of the stream. Little is known about spawning behavior in bigeye, gravel, and streamline chubs.

Gravel, streamline, and shoal chubs feed over clean sand and gravel, consuming a wide variety of aquatic insects. Gravel and shoal chubs also have cutaneous taste buds, present on the head and body, which they use to locate food. Streamline and bigeye chubs are sight feeders. River and hornyhead chubs consume a variety of plant and animal material, especially small crayfish. Adult creek chubs primarily eat fish but will also eat any other prey they can swallow.

Dace

Small, isolated, and often shallow pools in headwater streams with overhanging vegetation would seem one of the last places to find a vibrant fish community. In these isolated pools, however, can be found some of Ohio's most colorful fishes. Five species of dace belonging to three genera inhabit these streams. Breeding male southern redbelly dace (genus *Phoxinus*), are spectacular—with yellow fins and bright red bellies contrasted by two black bands on the sides separated by yellow or white. Beautiful redside dace (genus *Clinostomus*), are marked by a deep red lateral band bordered with streaks of gold, and the similar rosyside dace sports a yellow-orange lateral band. Less colorful blacknose dace (genus *Rhinichthys*) are often marked with a bright orange lateral stripe.

The genus *Rhinicthys* is represented by the longnose and blacknose dace, which have stout, cylindrical bodies with down-turned mouths and long, pointed snouts. Of all Ohio's fish, longnose dace have one of the widest ranges, extending across Canada and the northern United States. In Ohio, they were originally only known in Lake Erie and the Chagrin River. In the 1980s, new populations were discovered in high-gradient Ohio River tributaries in Jefferson and Belmont Counties. There are also recent collections from similar tributaries in Columbiana County. There are marked color differences between the Lake Erie and Ohio River populations. The Lake Erie species appear silvery, while the Ohio River populations are gold. Both blacknose and longnose dace inhabit the riffles and runs of high-gradient streams, with the blacknose more abundant in small headwater tributaries.

Rosyside and redside dace, in the genus *Clinostomus*, have laterally compressed bodies, pointed snouts, and protruding jaws. Rosyside dace are restricted to clear headwater streams in Pike, Scioto, and Adams Counties. Surveys taken during the 1980s documented populations in forty streams (Rice and Phinney 1985). According to Brian Zimmerman, recent surveys have raised this total to almost sixty (personal communication). Redside and southern redbelly dace are found in high-gradient stream pools along the Allegheny Escarpment from Coshocton County north to Ashtabula County. There are also disjunct populations in the Mad River drainage in west-central Ohio, Hocking County, and Ohio River tributary streams in eastern Ohio from Washington County northward.

Dace are primarily insectivorous. Southern redbelly dace consume algae, diatoms, and detritus in addition to aquatic insects. Redside and rosyside dace are active predators, feeding on a variety of aquatic and terrestrial insects. These rover predators feed heavily on terrestrial insects, often jumping out of the water to snag a meal. Longnose and blacknose dace feed on more benthic organisms, consuming a variety of aquatic insects. Spawning males usually defend small territories established over sand or gravel. Longnose dace, in particular, are known for their aggressive behavior before spawning. They also employ a strange courtship ritual, in which the male will stick his long fleshy snout between two rocks and cause its snout and body to quiver. This seems to excite the female and initiates spawning. Breeding redside dace form tight schools with females on their outer margins. When ready to mate, a female will split off from the group, followed by several males. Mating and egg-laying (up to three hundred eggs) usually occurs over a creek chub nest. Spawning southern redbelly dace also use nests excavated by creek chubs. Males typically display no territorial defense; single females have been observed mating with two males simultaneously. During periods of low rainfall, dace and other resident species are often trapped in isolated pools. Competition for food in these dace holes is intense, with the young and weak often perishing.

Spectacular redside dace get their name from the brilliant red lateral bands seen on breeding males. They inhabit small, high-gradient tributaries throughout eastern Ohio.

Blacknose dace are identified by their round bodies and overhanging snouts. Inhabiting small, high-gradient tributaries throughout much of Ohio, they are more tolerant of turbid water than other dace. Breeding males are identified by orange lateral bands.

During the breeding season, male fathead minnow heads begin to enlarge. One of the state's most pollution-tolerant species, the fathead minnow is widespread throughout glaciated Ohio.

Breeding male stonerollers are Ohio's most colorful minnows. Fins are streaked with vivid black, orange, and tan markings, which contrast with white lips. Numerous sharp white tubercles cover the head and body.

The suckermouth minnow is a prairie stream species that invaded Ohio from the west as original forests were cleared. Tolerant of turbid water, it is found in larger streams, where it frequents riffles and runs.

One of Ohio's most common species, the creek chub is abundant in small tributaries. Females and young have small pre-caudal spots. Small scales and a large terminal mouth help identify this relatively nondescript species.

Found in small streams throughout the state, stonerollers like this juvenile are one of Ohio's most commonly encountered fish. A round snout, subterminal mouth, and dark spots that resemble missing body scales are diagnostic field marks.

Breeding male southern redbelly dace are among the most colorful of the state's fishes. Common inhabitants of small headwater streams, they are widely distributed throughout southwestern and eastern Ohio.

Gravel chubs are identified by their large eyes, rounded bodies, and the W- or X-shaped markings found on their back and sides. Inhabitants of the larger streams, like the Muskingum and Scioto Rivers, they are found in swift current over gravel runs.

Sight feeders requiring clear water, bigeye chubs have been expanding their range since the mid-1990s in the Muskingum and Scioto drainages.

Stonerollers are herbivores, grazing on algae and other plant material. Large numbers can sometimes be taken in riffles and runs enriched by growths of filamentous green algae.

Endangered pugnose minnows get their name from their rounded snouts and small oblique mouths. This clear-water species is restricted to a few glacial lakes and the St. Marys River.

Males of many species of cyprinids, like these bluntnose minnows, develop tubercles during the breeding season. Breeding males darken in color, their heads becoming almost black.

Stout-bodied bullhead minnows look similar to bluntose minnows. Inhabitants of large rivers, each has a dark crescent-shaped spot between the jaw and eye.

Longnose dace are identified by their elongated snouts, which overhang their lower jaws. Dusky scales scattered over the back and upper sides give this species a mottled appearance. They can be found under rocks in high-gradient riffles in the Chagrin River and a few eastern Ohio tributaries.

Rosyside dace are restricted to small, high-gradient tributaries in southern Ohio. Similar in appearance to redside dace, they are deep-bodied and lack protruding lower jaws.

Creek chubs like this large male are frequently caught by trout anglers. Breeding males are flushed with blue, green, and rose.

During the breeding season, river chub male heads enlarge and are covered with breeding tubercles. The swollen heads are thought to aid in the movement of gravel when constructing nests.

Aptly named male hornyhead chubs develop swollen heads covered with many tubercles, or nodes. Dark carmine spots behind the eyes can be observed on most breeding males.

River chubs inhabit riffles and runs of large rivers and streams throughout the state. Sensitive to silted substrate, they have disappeared from many of their former haunts.

The bluntnose minnow is an abundant Ohio species. Easily identified by their black lateral lines and dorsal fin spots, these fish reach their greatest abundance in ponded streams.

Hornyhead chubs inhabit headwater streams throughout glaciated Ohio. Both young and adults have dark lateral stripes and pre-caudal spots.

Streamline chubs have slender, rounded bodies and a series of black spots along their lateral lines. Their populations, originally restricted to a few high-quality streams like Big Darby Creek and the Kokosing and Walhonding Rivers, are expanding in the Scioto, Muskingum, and upper Ohio River drainages.

Western tongue-tied minnows get their name from their small, subterminal mouths. Populations are restricted to clear high-gradient streams of the upper Mad River in Logan, Champaign, and Clark Counties.

Shiners
Exploiting a Niche

CHAPTER 4

Have you ever looked down into a stream on a sunny afternoon and observed a silver flash like a mirror reflecting light? Closer examination will likely reveal a school of small fish moving over the rocky bottom. You are most likely looking at a school of shiners, a diverse group of relatively small and usually silver-sided fish belonging to the Family Cyprinidae. Comprising both habitat specialists and generalists, they are among the dominant members of the stream communities found in Ohio.

Among the cyprinids in the state, there are five genera of shiners (*Notropis, Cyprinella, Lythrurus, Luxilus,* and *Notemigonus*). Collectively, these include more than 140 North American species. The *Notropis,* or eastern shiners, with more than 90 species (16 in Ohio) are the second largest genus of freshwater fish on the continent. All are small, rarely exceeding four inches in length. The Cyprinellids, or satinfin shiners, number 30 species, 2 found in Ohio. A distinctive crosshatching pattern formed by the scales above and below their lateral line helps identify them. The 2 Ohio species of *Lythrurus,* or fine-scaled shiners, are distinguished by scales that are hard to discern with the naked eye. The *Luxilus,* or high-scaled shiners (2 in Ohio), are characterized by their slab-sided bodies and large scales, which fall off if carelessly handled. High-scale shiners are larger than most other Ohio species; the striped shiner exceeds nine inches. The genus *Notemigonus* includes a single species, the golden shiner. A slab-sided fish characterized by a small triangular-shaped head, it can be more than ten inches long.

Historically there were twenty-three species of shiners recorded in Ohio. One of North America's rarer shiners, the pugnose has not been collected on the Ohio side of Lake Erie since 1931 and is now considered extirpated. Two other species, the blacknose and blackchin, have not been found in recent years and are also considered extirpated from the state. Of the remaining twenty, three are listed as either endangered or threatened. Popeye shiners, a southern species, have been known historically from an 1898 collection in the Maumee River and was thought to be absent from Ohio until a new population was discovered in 1984 in Scioto Brush Creek in southern Ohio. Threatened bigeye shiners can still be found in a few clear-water streams in southern Ohio, including Sunfish, Turkey, and White Oak Creeks. The Black and Rocky Rivers have a small disjunct population of bigmouth shiners, probably isolated by the last glacial event. The nearest populations of this prairie stream species are found in Indiana. Other disjunct populations occur in western Michigan, western New York, Pennsylvania, and northern West Virginia.

In Ohio, the greatest diversity of shiners often occurs in larger rivers. Like darters, shiners have evolved to fill a variety of habitats. Habitat variables include the type of water body, stream gradient, substrate composition, water clarity, water temperature, and presence of aquatic vegetation. Common names of some species reflect their habitat preferences. River and channel shiners, for example, are inhabitants of large rivers, and sand shiners are associated with sandy substrates. Sand shiners are one of North America's most abundant species; populations are found across the eastern United States, extending as far west as the Rocky Mountains. Bigeye and popeye shiners are large-eyed sight feeders limited to waters of great clarity.

Shiners primarily inhabit pools, backwaters, and other areas of moderate current. A few species, like emerald and spottail shiners, which can tolerate turbid waters, are common in Lake Erie, where sport anglers use them as bait. Other species that formerly inhabited the lake, such as pugnose and blackchin shiners, disappeared in the nineteenth century as turbidity levels increased. The golden shiner, another inhabitant of clear weedy lakes and streams, reaches its greatest abundance in northeast Ohio beaver floodings. A few species, like channel and river shiners, are restricted to the Ohio River and its larger tributaries. Emerald shiners, which also inhabit large rivers, are one of the most abundant fish in the Mississippi River system. Ghost shiners, formerly restricted to the Ohio River and its larger tributaries, are now well established in the Maumee River. All of these are tolerant of the turbid conditions found in these large rivers.

A few species reach their greatest numbers in small headwater tributaries. Scarlet shiners, found in central and southern Ohio streams, require clear water and deep pools. Closely related redfin shiners, found in northern and southeastern Ohio, can tolerate more turbid conditions. Striped and common shiners, two of our largest species also inhabit small to moderate-sized streams. Since the early twentieth century, striped shiners have gradually spread eastward, hybridizing with common shiners. Today common shiners are limited to isolated tributaries above dams and waterfalls. Many of the state's common species, like spotfin, sand, mimic, rosyface and silver shiners, occur over a wider range of stream sizes. Silver and rosyface shiners are two species that favor the stronger currents found at the foot of riffles and runs in moderate to large streams.

The diversity and abundance of shiners in riverine systems, coupled with their differing sensitivities to water quality and habitat degradation, makes them excellent barometers of stream health. Species requiring clear waters and beds of aquatic vegetation, like the pugnose and blackchin shiners, were some of the first fish to disappear from Ohio waters. Blacknose and bigeye shiners, though never common, have also disappeared from much of their former range. Generalists like redfin, striped, spotfin, and steelcolor shiners, as well as the silverjaw minnow (a shiner in the genus *Notropis*), show wider tolerances to increased water turbidity and remain common species within their Ohio ranges. Sand and mimic shiners are also not affected by increased turbidities as long as sand and gravel substrates remain free of silt. Rosyface and silver shiners require clear, fast-moving water but, perhaps because of their association with swift currents, show some tolerance to moderate levels of turbidity.

During the breeding season many shiners exhibit sexual dimorphism. Males will develop breeding tubercles that cover their heads. The role of these tubercles during spawning is still uncertain; they may help the male hold the females during spawning or serve as a warning to rival males and potential mates about the overall fitness of the individual. In addition to tubercles, males of many species become brightly colored during the breeding season. These colors give many shiners their common names. Rosyface, redfin, scarlet, steelcolor, and golden shiners are some of Ohio's most beautiful species. Spotfin shiners get their name from the dark spot on their dorsal fins, and silver and emerald shiners are named for their overall coloration.

There have been relatively few detailed studies of shiner spawning behavior. Many shiners are broadcast spawners, releasing their fertilized eggs over sand and gravel substrates. Sand, bigmouth, silver, mimic, and spottail shiners are all thought to spawn this way. Several species of broadcast spawners, such as emerald and redfin shiners, form large schools of spawning adults. Blackchin and golden shiners, inhabitants of weedy glacial lakes, broadcast their eggs over beds of aquatic vegetation. Golden shiners have also been observed spawning over nests excavated by bluegill and largemouth bass. When spawning over nests excavated by longear sunfish, territorial male redfins defend these sites from other males of their species. Scarlet shiners have also been observed spawning over nests excavated by sunfish and creek chubs. Steelcolor and spotfin shiners are crevice spawners, depositing their eggs under logs and other woody debris or in cracks between rocks. Males in this group are strongly territorial. While many other cyprinids build nests for spawning, only a few of the shiners do so. Striped and common shiners typically use nests excavated by creek chubs. Breeding males are territorial and defend both nests and eggs.

Shiners are primarily insectivorous. Zooplankton, small crustaceans, and aquatic and terrestrial insects are important prey items. Adult shiners use caddisfly, mayfly, stonefly, and midge larvae, and juveniles take smaller prey items, such as zooplankton, cladocerans, copepods, and midge larvae. There are often seasonal differences in available prey. Some species will also ingest small amounts of algae, detritus, and other organic matter when prey items become scarce. Rosyface and spotfin shiners will take terrestrial insects from the water's surface, sometimes leaping into the air to catch them. Golden shiners have perhaps the most interesting feeding strategy of any shiner; they consume a wide variety of insects, zooplankton, algae, and plant material. Capable of filter feeding on zooplankton, they are also efficient sight feeders, eating aquatic insects when available. Many river species congregate into large feeding schools, moving into shallow waters at night to forage over sand and gravel substrates. It is not uncommon in these instances to capture a thousand individuals at one time in a six-by-ten–foot seine. In Lake Erie, large schools of emerald shiners follow the diurnal movements of the zooplankton on which they feed, rising to the surface at night to feed then retiring to the depths during daylight hours.

Ohio shiners present many identification challenges for fish enthusiasts. Looking superficially alike, mimic, sand, and channel shiners are especially hard to separate in the field. Highly variable mimic shiners present the most problems and are best identified in the laboratory. The morphology of the head as it relates to the shape and positioning of the mouth can help with identifying different species and understanding their feeding strategies. Species with obliquely upturned mouths, such as the blackchin and pugnose shiners, tend to forage on or near the surface. Those with subterminal

Spottail shiners are slab-sided and look similar to silver shiners. Formerly restricted to Lake Erie, they have been introduced into several reservoirs in northeast Ohio. Populations are also established in the Mahoning and upper Ohio River basins.

mouths, such as the sand, mimic, bigmouth, and silverjaw minnows, are primarily bottom-feeders. The majority have terminal mouths, which allow them to take prey from the surface as well as the bottom. Many species are primarily sight feeders, which explains their general intolerance of turbid waters. In this most interesting family of fishes, each species has adapted to exploit a particular habitat, as evidenced by differences in morphological and behavioral characteristics.

Emerald shiners are abundant in Lake Erie and Ohio River drainages. Lacking distinctive markings, young can be difficult to distinguish from other shiners.

Breeding tubercles are easily seen on large species like the striped shiner. On smaller shiners, they are usually too small to see with the naked eye.

Silverjaw minnows inhabit a range of stream sizes but reach their greatest abundance in small tributaries. They can tolerate pollution, including mine wastes, as long as substrates remain clean.

Intense colors, tubercles, and a slab-sided body identify this breeding striped shiner.

Endangered popeye shiners are found only in Sunfish and Scioto Brush Creeks in southern Ohio. This pool-dwelling species requires clear waters and silt-free substrates.

Sand shiners are one of Ohio's most common and widely distributed species. Foraging over sandy substrates, they are hard to separate from other shiners that often join them in mixed schools.

Common shiners are restricted to headwater streams across northern Ohio. They are threatened by expanding populations of striped shiners, which freely interbreed with them, creating many hybrids.

Silverjaw minnows are named for prominent platelike divisions present on the upper and lower jaws. Large eyes, rounded snouts, and subterminal mouths are other identifying field marks.

Blacknose shiners occupy the same habitats as blackchin shiners. Formerly widespread in glaciated Ohio, they were last collected in Rocky Fork Creek in Franklin County; like blackchins, they are now gone from the state.

Channel shiners inhabit Ohio's largest rivers. In the field, they are hard to distinguish from other shiners.

Populations of threatened bigmouth shiners inhabit the Black and Rocky Rivers in northern Ohio. They are disjunct from western populations, which were separated during the last glacial event.

The threatened bigeye shiner is a pool species that requires clear water. Small populations remain in southern Ohio in Turkey, Sunfish, and White Oak Creeks.

Blackchin shiners are residents of clear weedy glacial lakes. Last collected in Meyers Lake, Stark County, in the early 1980s, this species is now considered extirpated from Ohio. This fish can be identified by the lateral dusky stripe that crosses the eye, snout, and chin.

Rosyface shiners are named for the red that colors the heads of breeding males. Sleek and agile, they inhabit the fast currents of riffles and runs in large streams.

Mimic shiners frequent larger streams, where they often school with sand shiners. Though these fish are hard to distinguish from sand shiners, their anal ray counts and raised lateral line scales help identify them.

Scarlet shiners get their name from the red coloring that infuses the fins of breeding males. They look similar to redfin shiners, but for their thinner bodies. They are found in small clear streams in southwestern Ohio.

Golden shiners are common inhabitants of beaver swamps and ponded streams with aquatic vegetation. Small heads and slab-sided bodies help identify these large shiners.

The steelcolor shiner is found in the Ohio drainage, seldom east of the Scioto River. Inhabiting large pools, it commonly associates with the very similar spotfin shiner. Differences in the number of anal rays help separate the two species.

The silver shiners lack the distinctive breeding colors displayed by many Notropis species. Distinguished by large eyes and a pair of half-moon–shaped bars on the top of their heads, they are a pool-dwelling species found in large rivers.

Spotfin shiners are common in larger streams throughout the state. Their terminal mouths allow them to take prey from the water's surface.

Abundant striped shiners inhabit rivers of all sizes throughout Ohio. They are particularly common in small streams.

Redfin shiners get their name from the red that infuses the fins of breeding males. Like those of many species of cyprinids, breeding males of this species develop small tubercles on their faces and heads.

Translucent ghost shiners are one of Ohio's smaller shiners. Good numbers of them can be found in the Maumee, Muskingum, and Ohio Rivers.

Suckers
Swimming against the Current

CHAPTER 5

Suckers are among the most maligned freshwater fish in North America. Anglers often refer to these as "rough" fish; subterminal mouths coupled with intramuscular bones make them difficult to catch and eat. Nonetheless, suckers are important to healthy stream ecosystems. Many species are sensitive to pollution and serve as important barometers of water quality. Their young are also an important prey item for many larger fish.

Suckers comprise the Catostomidae, a group encompassing more than seventy-five species, of which all but one are confined to North America and eastern Siberia. The word "Catostomidae" means "inferior mouth" and refers to the position of the mouth on the underside of the head. In the majority of suckers, fleshy protrusible lips thicken the mouth. The fish pick, or "suck," benthic organisms off bottom substrates with these lips. Their scaleless heads, reflecting cycloid scales, and silver or gold coloring are other identifying features. They have soft-rayed fins that lack sharp spines, and all have rows of sixteen or more pharyngeal teeth. In some species, these resemble molars and are used for crushing snails and other hard-bodied prey, especially small crustaceans.

Ohio has been home to twenty-one of the approximately forty species of suckers found in the eastern United States. These represent seven of the thirteen genera comprising the Family Catostomidae. The largest eastern genus, the *Moxostoma* or redhorse suckers, represent twenty-three species, of which eight are known from Ohio. Redhorses are large, round-bodied fish with large highly reflective scales. The *Catostomus,* the largest genus in the family, having twenty-seven species, is, with two exceptions (longnose and white suckers), largely western in distribution. These species are distinguished by their small, non-reflective scales. Other important Ohio genera include *Carpiodes* (carpsuckers) and *Ictiobus* (buffalofish), with three species each. Members of both genera are large, deep-bodied, laterally compressed fish with large, reflective scales. Carpsuckers are primarily silver, and buffalofish are more black or bluish. The remaining genera represented in Ohio are *Erimyzon* (chubsucker), with two species; and *Hypentelium* (hogsucker), *Minytrema* (spotted sucker), and *Cycleptus* (blue sucker), with one species each.

The harelip sucker has the distinction of being the first fish to become extinct in the United States. Though widely distributed in clear water streams of the southern and midwestern states before the turn of the twentieth century, it was last collected in Ohio's Banchard and Auglaize Rivers in 1893. Anglers called this moxostomid, historically common in the Scioto River, the May sucker, in reference to its spring spawning runs. Its small mouth and tight gill covers are thought to have made it particularly vulnerable to asphyxiation from the silts and colloidal clays being transported in ever greater amounts by rivers and streams as riparian flood plains were cleared for agriculture.

Of twenty sucker species still inhabiting Ohio waters, the longnose is listed as endangered, and the blue sucker, greater redhorse, and lake chubsucker are currently threatened. Longnose suckers have one of the widest distributions of all the catostomids encompassing most of Alaska, Canada, and the northern United States. The state's population is restricted to Lake Erie, where commercial fishing has provided most records from the deep water of the eastern basin. In the nineteenth century, blue suckers were common in the Ohio River and the lower sections of the larger tributaries, like the Muskingum and Scioto Rivers. Dam construction and substrate siltation have eliminated or severely depressed Ohio River populations. The few recent records have been from swift-riffle complexes in the lower reaches of the Great Miami, Little Miami, and Scioto Rivers. The lower Scioto has been particularly favorable for this species in recent years.

Historically, greater redhorses inhabited the larger streams of the Maumee drainage in northwest Ohio. Recent fieldwork by the Ohio EPA and others has discovered small populations still persisting in the Sandusky, Auglaize, Tiffin, and St. Joseph Rivers in northwestern Ohio. Lake chubsuckers inhabit pothole lakes and ponded streams, characterized by clear water and submerged vegetation. A relict species, they are locally distributed throughout the state, found in a number of glacial lakes and habitats associated with the upper Cuyahoga River. Habitat destruction has resulted in the extirpation of many populations, like those found in Buckeye Lake and Sandusky Bay. New populations were documented in a number of Teays-age wetlands and other ponded stream habitats in Jackson, Gallia, and Lawrence Counties during surveys Dan Rice and George Phinney conducted there in the 1980s. The only other Ohio sucker sharing this same habitat is the spotted sucker. This southern species favors ponded headwater streams like the upper Cuyahoga River. Recent surveys in Ohio's glacial lakes by Brian Zimmerman also documented populations in most of these lakes (personal communication).

Almost all Ohio's suckers are riverine, utilizing deeper pools in areas of moderate current. With the exception of the white sucker and creek chubsucker, they are generally absent from small streams. White suckers are the state's most abundant species, inhabiting both lakes and streams. Hogsuckers are found in streams throughout the state, inhabiting the swift currents of riffles and runs. Aerodynamically designed, with large pectoral fins, depressed heads, and streamlined bodies, they sit motionless on the bottom, seemingly pinned by the force of the water. When wading in fast riffles, an observant angler will see this distinctive species darting from underfoot; a large head and dark saddle bands make them easily identifiable. Creek chubsuckers are found in ponded headwaters. Once widespread in the clear prairie streams of western Ohio, these fish disappeared from much of their former range because of habitat destruction and increasing water turbidities. Small populations can still be found in the Blanchard River and other tributaries of the Maumee. Populations also persist in tributaries of the Great and Little Miami River systems. Surveys by Rice and Hoggarth have also demonstrated an unexpected but wide-ranging presence in the Pine Creek system in Lawrence and Scioto Counties.

Golden redhorses are Ohio's most abundant moxostomid; they appear more tolerant of increased water turbidity than other members of the genus. All moxostomids have small mouths and tight gill covers and are sensitive to excessive siltation and pollution. Silver redhorses are found in larger streams with moderate gradients, where they inhabit deep pools. Black redhorses favor the swift currents associated with riffles and runs. Smallmouth redhorses of the Ohio River drainage and shorthead redhorses of the Lake Erie drainage share the same habitat requirements with other family members. They were thought the same species until recent taxonomic studies determined them separate ones. Shorthead redhorses are common in Lake Erie, where they once represented a significant part of the commercial catch. Among suckers, they were second only to the white in their importance to this fishery.

Carpsuckers and buffalofish are primarily inhabitants of the state's larger rivers. Quillback carpsuckers, found in both the Lake Erie and Ohio River drainages, are common and widespread in low-gradient streams and pools. Unlike river and highfin carpsuckers, which are big-river fish, quillbacks will ascend smaller tributaries to spawn. River and highfin carpsuckers, like quillbacks, are widespread throughout the Mississippi River drainage, including the Ohio and its larger tributaries, backwaters, and oxbows. Quillbacks can tolerate turbid conditions and seem less affected by silt deposition. Buffalofish are also residents of Ohio's largest rivers: Black and smallmouth buffalos frequent deep pools with moderate to fast current. Bigmouth buffalos are found in backwaters associated with the state's largest rivers, like the Scioto, as well as Lake Erie.

Spawning generally begins in May, when water temperatures reach sixty degrees. Suckers are broadcast spawners, scattering their adhesive eggs over stream bottoms. River redhorses have been observed constructing nests, using their heads and caudal fins to excavate twelve-inch depressions (Hackney, Tatum, and Spencer 1968). River and shorthead females will often mate with two males simultaneously. Silver redhorses are highly migratory and seek deep riffles for spawning. Bigmouth buffalo form spawning groups usually composed of three to five males for every female, whose egg-laying induces the attending males to release milt at the same time. Females can produce prodigious numbers of eggs; one large female in a Canadian study held an estimated 750,000 (Johnson 1963). Chubsuckers, spotted suckers, and some redhorses have been observed defending loosely defined spawning territories. The movement of a receptive female into one of these territories initiates spawning. Males in these species develop breeding tubercles on their heads, a trait lacking in many of the nonterritorial species, like carpsuckers and buffalofish. River carpsuckers also form large spawning aggregations, with large females producing more than 100,000 eggs (Mayhew 1987). In spring, bigmouth and smallmouth buffalos move into shallow backwaters and flooded lowlands to spawn. White suckers move into headwater tributaries in the spring, when small holes can be filled with breeding adults.

Suckers eat a variety of aquatic macroinvertebrates especially small crustaceans and mollusks. River redhorses feed almost exclusively on snails and mollusks, using their molarlike pharyngeal teeth to crush hard shells. Many suckers are thought primarily sight feeders. In turbid conditions, bottom-feeding suckers rely on their senses of touch and taste, found on their protrusible lips. Buffalofish can also use their thin comblike pharyngeal teeth to filter algae and zooplankton from turbid water. Young bigmouth buffalo have been found feeding primarily on zooplankton, and adults eat macroinvertebrates. Suckers often forage together in large schools. It is not uncommon to catch four species of redhorse in a day's seining. The loss of clean substrates that support communities of aquatic invertebrates has played an important role in the decline of Ohio sucker populations.

Suckers were once part of thriving commercial fishery businesses in both Lake Erie and the Ohio River. Redhorses and white suckers were sold under the name "mullet." Blue suckers were also highly desirable, and bigmouth buffalo were considered important enough to be stocked in Lake Erie. Lengths of three feet have been reported for blue suckers, though such large specimens are a rarity today. Buffalofish were also important to commercial fisheries on the Ohio River, with large bigmouth buffalos topping sixty pounds. Shorthead redhorses were once a valuable commercial species in Lake Erie, where they attained lengths of two feet and weights of four to six pounds. Public taste has gradually turned away from suckers as a food source, and few people now will admit to eating them. With few laws currently protecting this unique family of fishes, suckers are indeed swimming against the current of public opinion.

One of Ohio's most common suckers, the golden redhorse inhabits larger streams throughout Ohio. A fleshy subterminal mouth and cylindrical body with large reflective scales help to identify the redhorse sucker.

Hogsuckers are readily identified by their flattened heads, downward sloping snouts, and suckerlike mouths with protruding lips. From the front, a northern hogsucker's face looks similar to a pig's. Unique from other Ohio suckers, it has a depression between its eyes.

A southern species, the spotted sucker lacks large reflective scales. These fish are locally distributed in Ohio and inhabit a variety of lentic waters, especially ponded streams.

Restricted to high-quality streams, silver redhorses inhabit deeper pools, often schooling with other redhorse species. Small mouths and tight gill covers make redhorses vulnerable to asphyxiation from silted water.

Similar in appearance to shorthead redhorses, smallmouth redhorses inhabit large streams in the Ohio River drainage. Small heads and scarlet tailfins help identify them.

One of Ohio's most common species (also its most common sucker), the white sucker inhabits streams of all sizes. Small, nonreflective scales distinguish it from the redhorse sucker. Breeding adults have rosy lateral stripes.

Inhabitants of fast currents, hogsuckers are found statewide. They are often observed darting from underfoot when disturbed.

Creek chubsuckers are found in small ponded streams in western Ohio. Drainage projects have eliminated most of this prairie stream species' habitat.

Common quillback carpsuckers inhabit streams statewide. Their deep bodies, elongated dorsal fin rays, and silvery scales help identify them. Young carpsuckers are hard to identify to the species level in the field.

Threatened lake chubsuckers are inhabitants of glacial lakes and other lentic waters supporting growths of aquatic vegetation. Black lateral bands distinguish young chubsuckers.

Northern hogsuckers are easily identified by their large triangular heads and dusky saddle bands. In spring, members of this common species migrate into smaller tributaries to spawn.

Shorthead redhorses are common in Lake Erie and its tributaries. Their small heads and red tails help differentiate them from other redhorse species.

Catfish
Night Stalkers

CHAPTER 6

Ictaluridae is one of the largest families of freshwater fish found in North America, with about fifty species among seven genera. Four genera represent the eastern United States: *Ictalurus* (channel, or fork-tailed, catfish), *Ameiurus* (bullheads), *Pylodictis* (flathead catfish), and *Noturus* (madtoms). All are easily identified by smooth, scaleless skin; four pairs of barbels, or whiskers, on the chin and upper jaw; and sharp spines on dorsal and pectoral fins. Any fisherman who has caught a catfish learns to respect these spines; particularly those sported by the madtoms. If carelessly handled, madtoms can deliver a venomous sting similar to that of a bee or wasp. Members of this family are also identified by their slightly flattened heads and the small, fleshy adipose fins on the dorsal surfaces of their bodies. Catfish are primarily active at night, moving onto riffles and shoals to feed. Photoreceptors in the fish's eyes gather ambient light, which shines onto the fishes' retinas, enabling them to see in almost total darkness. With receptors on their barbels and lips, they have a highly developed sense of smell, evidenced by the variety of stinkbaits anglers use to attract them. While they can be captured during daylight hours, the serious angler waits until dark. For a biologist standing in a riffle at night with a seine full of fish, glowing eyes reflected in the headlamp mean catfish.

At thirty species, madtoms are the most diverse and interesting members of the family. They are small fish adapted to a variety of stream habitats whose cryptic coloring camouflages them from predators. Differentiating among the different species can be difficult, but identifying characteristics include differences in pigmentation patterns and shape and size of pectoral and dorsal fins. Many have limited ranges and, like the darters and shiners, exhibit a high degree of endemism, particularly in the southern United States. Limited ranges and an intolerance of pollution and habitat degradation have resulted in no fewer than five species being listed as federally endangered. Ohio has one of these, the Scioto madtom, known only in a single riffle complex in lower Big Darby Creek. Only twenty-three individuals have ever been captured, the last specimens collected in 1957.

In addition to the Scioto, five other species of madtoms are known in the state. Northern madtoms are currently listed as state endangered, and the mountain madtom is listed as threatened. Increasing populations of mountain madtoms were identified in the Muskingum and Little Miami Rivers in the 1980s and 1990s. More recently, this species has been expanding its range in both systems and has also been reported from other drainages. Northern madtoms are found in small numbers in the main stem of the Muskingum River and in other widely scattered locales, like Big Darby Creek in central Ohio and the Whitewater River in southwestern Ohio. Madtoms hide under rocks or bury themselves in loose gravel, only coming out at night to forage. Stonecats are Ohio's largest madtom, sometimes twelve inches long. Their common name comes from their habit of hiding under flat rocks in large streams. Stonecats also inhabit rocky shorelines and reefs in Lake Erie, where wave actions and currents mimic stream conditions. Ranging statewide, brindled madtoms are inhabitants of low-gradient riffles and pools, where they are commonly found hiding in woody debris, leaves, and undercut banks. Like mountain and northern madtoms, brindleds are more easily captured in the fall. Tadpole madtoms favor quiet pools with rooted aquatic vegetation and organic debris; they also inhabit weedy glacial lakes, river oxbows, and other wetlands. Their populations are now greatly reduced by habitat destruction.

When spawning, female madtoms attach sticky eggs to the underside of rocks and woody debris. They also use man-made objects, like broken crockery. Crayfish burrows and discarded beverage cans also make suitable homes for brindled and tadpole madtoms. Northern, mountain, and stonecat madtoms prefer flat rocks in riffles. Males of all species guard their eggs and young until they disperse from the nest site. Diets include a variety of aquatic insect larvae and microcrustaceans. Adult stonecats also prey on small fish, worms, and hellgrammites.

Unlike madtoms, which favor rocky riffles and runs, bullheads in the genus *Ameiurus* are inhabitants of river pools and lakes. Ohio is home to three of the seven species in this genus: yellow, black, and brown bullheads.

All appear to occupy a similar ecological niche, favoring vegetated embayments of Lake Erie, inland lakes, stream pools, and river oxbows. Abundant yellow bullheads also can be found in many of the state's smaller rivers and streams, where they often hide below undercut banks, roots, and woody debris. Brown bullheads like deeper vegetated waters, and there are isolated populations in some of the state's larger glacial lakes. Black bullheads favor warm, shallow, turbid water; they are common in Lake Erie, where they inhabit muddy or silted bottoms. Black bullheads have historically been restricted to the Ohio River drainage. The canal system built in the 1830s connecting Lake Erie to the Ohio River joined isolated populations of black and brown bullheads. Later, state stocking programs further mixed these two species, resulting in much hybridizing.

Bullheads, like other members of the family, nest in natural cavities in stream banks or fashion circular depressions under roots, submerged timber, or rocks or in hollow stumps. Brown bullheads are known to lay as many as thirteen thousand eggs. One or both sexes will remain to guard the eggs and young. Newly hatched bullheads aggregate into large feeding balls. Looking very much like schools of tadpoles, these can be observed wandering aimlessly near the surface, accompanied by an adult. Bullheads are omnivorous, consuming a variety of plant and animal material; as bottom feeders, their entire bodies are covered with sensory organs that help locate food.

Bullheads can tolerate high levels of pollution. Black bullheads, in particular, can survive in degraded waters toxic to other species. Bullheads, like other species of catfish, are renowned for their ability to survive for long periods of time out of water; every angler has a story of throwing a catfish into his trunk only to find it still moving several hours later. The ability to survive in polluted waters and bottom-dwelling habits has earned bullheads a less than desirable reputation among anglers. Nonetheless, they are important as sport fish: large ones can be more than eighteen inches long.

Blue and channel catfish in the genus *Ictalurus* are two of the largest members of the family. Blue catfish, which can weigh more than one hundred pounds, are restricted to the Ohio River, where they inhabit deep pools. At night, they move onto shallow riffles and bars to feed. Navigation dams built on the Ohio River eliminated much of their original habitat, and they are now considered rare. Channel catfish are still common in the Ohio River and elsewhere throughout the state, including Lake Erie. Like blue catfish, these favor deep pools in larger streams. In spring, adults move into small tributaries to spawn. Channel catfish are mainly cavity nesters, using hollow stumps, submerged logs, and holes in riverbanks. Males guard the eggs and young until they are ready to leave the nest. Adults have a varied diet of aquatic insects, crayfish, mollusks, and small fish. Throughout Ohio, channel catfish are commonly stocked in impoundments, ponds, and lakes.

Distinctive flathead catfish have wide, flattened heads and yellow bodies mottled with dark blotches. They are equipped with large spines and venom glands that together can inflict a painful injury on an unwary angler. Originally reported from the Ohio River and its tributaries, flatheads are now found in most of Lake Erie's larger tributary streams. Active feeders, at night they move into shallow water, where they mainly consume live fish. Adults will aggressively defend their nests against intruders. Young consume a wide variety of aquatic insect larvae, fish, and crayfish. Introductions in some streams have decimated resident populations of other fish species. Large individuals can weigh more than fifty pounds and are top predators in the food chain.

At night, northern madtoms move into the shallows to feed. Populations of this rare madtom are hard to ascertain because of their nocturnal habits.

Standing water and soft bottoms in rivers, oxbows, swamps, and marshes are home to tadpole madtoms.

Brown bullheads prefer weedy lakes and ponded headwater streams as habitat.

Channel catfish begin spawning when water temperatures reach seventy degrees. Young look similar to adults.

Widely distributed brindled madtoms are found statewide. Like all madtoms, the brindled's sharp spines can give the unwary handler a painful sting.

Channel catfish are common in lakes and large rivers statewide. They are widely stocked in farm ponds but rarely reproduce in them.

Populations of mountain madtoms are increasing because of improved water quality in the Muskingum and Little Miami Rivers.

Pollution-tolerant black bullheads are especially common in Lake Erie.

During the day, common stonecat madtoms can be found hiding under large flat rocks in swift river currents. They come out at night in search of prey.

Yellow bullheads are found in ponded lakes and streams statewide. Four white barbels below the mouth help identify this common species.

Sticklebacks, Mudminnows, Pirate Perch, and Others
Life in Small Places

CHAPTER 7

Fish can be found in many different places: rivers, ponds, or creeks, for example. There are, however, other habitats, smaller, isolated, less obvious ones. These include springs and roadside ditches that are sometimes only a few inches deep. These small places might contain a number of unusual and interesting fish, including mudminnows, topminnows, killifish, pirate perch, trout-perch, grass pickerel, sticklebacks, sculpins, brook silversides, and brook trout.

Brook sticklebacks are one of Ohio's more distinctive and unusual species. The family to which they belong (Gasterostsidae) includes at least sixteen species, with the majority of the family inhabiting the world's oceans. Four freshwater species are native to North America; only the brook stickleback, in the genus *Culaea,* is found in Ohio. Brook sticklebacks are small fish, seldom reaching three inches. They are slab-sided, with elongated bodies tapering to narrow connections with the caudal fins. They lack scales and are characterized by four to six sharp dorsal spines with little or no connecting membrane. Sticklebacks prefer cool clear-water habitats with abundant growths of aquatic vegetation. Distributed across the northern United States and Canada, in Ohio they are at the southern edge of their range. Widely distributed in northeastern Ohio, local populations can also be found in spring-fed tributaries of the upper Mad River in west-central Ohio. Habitats can be ephemeral; sticklebacks may be abundant one year in a particular location and gone the next.

When courting, male sticklebacks establish territories in aquatic vegetation, in which they construct golf ball-sized nests. They glue these nests with sticky secretions produced by their kidneys, and they aggressively defend their territories against intruders of all species. When a female appears, the male will actively herd her into his nest and block the opening. Captive females will lay between fifty and a hundred eggs and then escape by breaking through the back of the nest. The male then enters the nest, fertilizes the eggs, and repairs the damage in anticipation of mating with another female. It will guard both eggs and young until they disperse. Brook sticklebacks are carnivorous, eating a variety of aquatic macroinvertebrates, terrestrial insects, fish eggs, and zooplankton. These popular aquarium fish are aggressive and require separation from other species.

Related to the pikes, central mudminnows prefer many of the same habitats sticklebacks do. They are usually found in vernal pools and small ponded streams with dense beds of aquatic vegetation. More tolerant of turbid conditions than sticklebacks, they are known for their ability to survive periods of low water by burrowing into soft sediment. When levels of dissolved oxygen are insufficient, mudminnows gulp air from the surface, thanks to gas-absorbing organs in their swim bladders. Mudminnows are robust fish with rounded caudal and dorsal fins. Large individuals can reach five inches. They use pectoral fins as limbs to climb through dense vegetation. Spawning occurs in April, when water temperatures reach fifty degrees. The females lay adhesive eggs, attaching them to aquatic plants, and the males fertilize each egg individually. Large females can lay more than two thousand eggs, and no parental care is provided for eggs or young. Mudminnows are long-lived: captive specimens reach nine years. Bottom feeders, they consume a variety of aquatic insects, snails, and other small organisms. They are widely distributed in lentic habitats throughout northern Ohio.

With only a handful of records from the Maumee drainage, the state endangered pirate perch has always been a rare species in Ohio. No collections of it had been made in Ohio since the 1940s until 2011, when Brian Zimmerman captured a single specimen in one of its historic sites in the upper Auglaize River (personal communication). Like mudminnows, they inhabit oxbows and sluggish pools in low-gradient streams. Hiding in woody debris and undercut banks, they are especially hard to seine. They have distinctive long, stocky bodies with rounded caudal, anal, and dorsal fins. A notable feature of pirate perch is the placement of the anus, or cloacal opening. Rather than being positioned posteriorly, behind the pelvic fins, as in almost every other species of fish, in the pirate perch, this opening is situated under the head. This odd realignment allows the spawning females to place eggs in dense root masses, which they probe with their heads in search of suitable sites. Pirate perch are most active at night, feeding on a variety of benthic invertebrates and small fish. Ditching and drainage projects throughout western Ohio have destroyed most of their former habitat.

A person unfamiliar with grass pickerels might mistake them for young northern pike or muskellunge. Similar in appearance to their larger cousins, they have cheeks and opercles completely covered by scales. These small members of the Family Esocidae are seldom longer than twelve inches. A common species, the grass pickerel is frequently found in beaver floodings and oxbows. As do other members of the family, grass pickerel spawn in early spring, broadcasting eggs over emergent vegetation in shallow water. In spite of their small size, they are aggressive predators, darting out from vegetation to snap up small fish or invertebrates.

Anyone who has waded through a quiet pool of a western Ohio stream might have observed small, peculiar-looking fish with flattened heads, lying below the water's surface. These are blackstripe topminnows, one of three species in the genus *Fundulus* found in Ohio. The largest of three genera in the family (Fudulidae), the genus comprises thirty-eight species referred to as topminnows and killifish. Easy to keep in aquariums, they are some of the most sought-after native species. Topminnows are characterized by upturned mouths and single posterior dorsal fins. Blackstripe topminnows are easily identified by a black lateral band that also extends across the eye and snout. They are especially common in old canal lakes and ponded habitats in the western half of the state. During the breeding season, paired males and females defend small territories from rival topminnows. Females lay up to thirty eggs singly on aquatic vegetation. Topminnows feed primarily from the surface, taking a variety of terrestrial and aquatic insects.

Ohio's other native *Fundulus* is divided into two subspecies, the eastern and western banded killifish. Endangered western banded killifish were historically found in the vegetated embayments of the western basin of Lake Erie. Today relict populations exist mainly in limestone sinkholes, or blue holes, of Erie and Sandusky Counties, and small populations can also be found in the channelized tributaries of the Portage River in Wood County. During the 1930s, eastern banded killifish, an Atlantic Slope species, were released into Ohio River tributaries in northwestern Pennsylvania. Ten years later they were well established in the Beaver River system, with the first Ohio specimens reported from Jefferson County soon after. Eastern banded killifish also began invading Lake Erie as the result of an expanding population in New York. Killifish are identified by their laterally compressed bodies and the series of vertical bars extending along their sides. Eastern banded killifish have more vertical bars and dorsal rays than their western cousins. A shallow water species, the killifish swims in schools only a few inches below the surface and feeds on plankton and a variety of terrestrial and aquatic insects. During spawning, the eggs are released and fertilized in clusters that develop sticky filaments that adhere to aquatic plants.

Brook silversides' feeding habits are similar to those of topminnows. They swim in schools near the water's surface, where they feed on a variety of aquatic and terrestrial insects. Efficient feeders, they have flattened heads and upturned mouths. Their beaklike snouts with slightly protruding lower jaws, slender elongated bodies, plus long anal fins, complete the picture of this distinctive and unusual fish. Brook silversides are pale green, with broad silvery bands running down their sides, and they rarely exceed four inches in length. Spawning occurs during the summer months over gravel or beds of aquatic vegetation. Females extrude eggs individually, and each comes attached to an adhesive filament that sticks to the first object it encounters. They may have the shortest life span of any Ohio fish, with most individuals living only one year. Large numbers can be found in some of the state's larger lakes and reservoirs as well as ponded streams. Brook silversides are particularly sensitive to siltation and other forms of pollution.

With large heads and fan-shaped pectoral fins, sculpins make an unforgettable impression. They belong to the Family Cottidae, which numbers some three hundred species. North America is home to over thirty-five freshwater species of sculpins, which are largely marine in nature. Two of these, the mottled and spoonhead sculpins, are inhabitants of Ohio's waters. Widespread in Ohio, mottled sculpins inhabit rocky riffles and runs of small, high-gradient streams. Their flattened heads and scaleless bodies combined with the absence of a swim bladder enable them to live in swift currents of spring-fed streams. A rare species, the spoonhead sculpin inhabits the deeper waters of Lake Erie. Only three specimens are known from Ohio, where they were last collected in 1950. Breeding mottled sculpins excavate nests under flat rocks, which males defend against rivals. To attract females, they employ a series of courtship displays involving headshaking, gill flaring, and body undulations. During spawning, the pair lies upside down in the nest, where the female attaches her eggs to the roof of the cavity as the male fertilizes them. The male then chases the female away, to prevent her from eating any of the eggs. Males can mate with multiple females. In one study, a male was observed mating with as many as ten females (Downhower and Brown 1980). Males will guard nest and eggs until all the young are ready to leave. Bottom feeders, they eat a variety of aquatic macroinvertebrates and an occasional small fish.

Brook trout, Ohio's only native trout species, were historically found in several small spring-fed tributaries of the Chagrin River in Geauga County and from a small, unspecified creek in Ashtabula County (Kirtland 1880). Most populations were probably extirpated by the beginning of the twentieth century. As early as 1868, brook trout were released into numerous streams throughout the state, in an effort to start additional populations. These were temporarily established only in spring-fed tributaries of the upper Mad River in central Ohio and Cold Creek in Erie County. The discovery of a small population in a small tributary of the Chagrin River in Geauga County in the 1970s led to further surveys, which identified a second site in the upper Chagrin River. Springs feeding these small tributaries help maintain the sixty-five-degree water temperatures required for successful spawning. After DNA testing showed these populations to be native, the Division of Wildlife initiated a project to reintroduce them into other northeast Ohio streams. Beginning in the late 1990s, young brook trout raised in hatcheries using brood stock from the two native populations were released into approximately twenty small streams, which has resulted in six additional self-sustaining populations. Feeding primarily on terrestrial insects, adults seldom exceed eight inches and can live about four years.

One of only two living members of the Percopsidae, trout-perch are widely distributed in the upper Midwest and across Canada. They have large heads and elongated translucent bodies marked on their upper sides with lateral rows of dark spots. Like trout they have a small adipose fin, and like perch they have ctenoid scales, which are rough to the touch. Small fish, they are seldom five inches long. Trout-perch are common in Lake Erie and the Grand River as well as in some low-gradient streams in southeastern Ohio, where they inhabit small pools usually below undercut banks. A variety of crustaceans, aquatic insects, mollusks, and small fish make up their diet. Trout-perch are broadcast spawners, scattering eggs over sand and gravel substrates. In the past, massive die-offs of post-spawning adults have been recorded in Lake Erie.

Threatened brook trout are found in cold headwater streams. A few native populations still survive in northeast Ohio. Reintroductions in the 1990s derived from this native stock have resulted in the establishment of additional populations.

Having extended their range westward, eastern banded killifish are especially common in Lake Erie. These colorful fish, while popular with aquarium enthusiasts, are now listed as an aquatic nuisance species in Ohio, making it illegal to keep them.

Pirate perch are found in debris-choked standing water. A single specimen of this rare fish, undocumented since the 1940s, was captured in the Auglaize River in 2011.

Thanks to their vascularized swim bladders, central mudminnows can survive in oxygen-depleted waters by gulping air. They are common in dense aquatic vegetation.

An aggressive predator, the grass pickerel darts from aquatic vegetation to catch passing prey. These fish are abundant in lakes and ponded streams.

Small populations of western banded killifish can still be found in a few unpolluted lakes and blue holes, as well as in channelized tributaries of the Portage River in Wood County.

Brook silversides are efficient surface feeders. These fish form large schools and are particularly sensitive to pollution.

Brook trout young, or fry, display markings similar to those of adults.

Blackstripe topminnows are easily identified by their single lateral stripes, flattened heads, and upturned mouths. Males and females look similar.

Mottled sculpin inhabit rocky riffles in small spring-fed streams. Their large heads and pectoral fins help identify them.

Brook sticklebacks can be found in ditches with only a few inches of water. This cold-water species is on the southern edge of its range in Ohio.

Translucent trout-perch are especially common in Lake Erie and its tributaries. Their large heads and mouths also help to identify them.

Sunfish and Bass
Metallic Iridescence

CHAPTER 8

Almost all of Ohio's native basses, crappies, and sunfish belong to the Family Centrarchidae, which has over thirty North American freshwater species. They are, with one exception, native to eastern North America, extending west as far as the Rocky Mountains. Their main center of distribution is the Mississippi River Basin, though a number of species, including the banded sunfishes, are found in Atlantic and Gulf Coast drainages. Popular as sport fish, they have been introduced throughout the country.

One of the defining characteristics of the Centrarchidae, painfully familiar to anglers, is a dorsal fin containing between six and thirteen spines. Sharp spines associated with the anal fins are also capable of inflicting painful wounds. Other family characteristics include ctenoid scales with toothed rear edges. Together, these make sunfish feel rough when handled. Members of the family are typically deep-bodied and laterally compressed, with the exception of the more robust basses. Ohio is home to fourteen species of centrarchids representing four genera. The genus *Lepomis,* identified by a prominent "ear," which extends back from the posterior margin of the opercle, or gill cover, is the largest genus, with eight species in Ohio. Many of these, particularly longear, pumpkinseed, and orange-spotted sunfish, are known for the metallic colors their breeding males exhibit. Black basses in the genus *Micropterus* include the familiar largemouth, smallmouth, and spotted basses, which are among Ohio's most popular sport fish. Rock bass in the genus *Ambloplites* and black and white crappies (*Pomoxis*) complete the list.

Most are widely distributed and common in their appropriate habitat. Pumpkinseeds, warmouth sunfish, and black crappies hide in submerged aquatic vegetation of wetlands, weedy glacial lakes, and embayments of Lake Erie. They can also be found in ponded and low-gradient sections of large streams in glaciated portions of the state. Warmouth are one of the state's uncommon sunfish and are primarily found in northeastern Ohio, especially the Upper Cuyahoga River. Relict populations also exist in many of the state's glacial lakes. Pumpkinseeds are abundant in the vegetated embayments of Lake Erie and in ponded streams and lakes across northern Ohio. They were commercially harvested in Lake Erie until the early twentieth century, when laws were passed prohibiting the taking of all bass and sunfish. In the past, pumpkinseeds were rare in southern Ohio. Unlike the warmouth, healthy populations gradually became established in old canal lakes, like Buckeye, Indian, and Grand Lake St. Marys.

Black crappies frequent many of the same habitats as pumpkinseeds. They were not recorded in the Ohio River drainage before 1920; since then, intensive stocking of the state's lakes and reservoirs has established large populations statewide. White crappies tolerate more turbid water than black ones. Under these conditions, with little competition from other sunfish, they can become abundant. Both species have also been extensively stocked throughout the state. Bluegill and largemouth bass also favor the lentic habitats found in the state's lakes and larger streams. Prior to 1900 they were part of an important commercial fishery in the larger canal lakes. Like crappies, both species were extensively stocked throughout the twentieth century.

Orange-spotted sunfish, a prairie stream species, moved into western Ohio as clear waters became turbid. These small sunfish are one of the state's most colorful species, with metallic blue males covered with brilliant orange spots. Pollution-tolerant green sunfish are also abundant, found in streams, ponds, lakes, and river oxbows. Having unusually large mouths, they can take larger prey than other similar-sized sunfish. Spotted bass are restricted to the Ohio River drainage, where they are common in our rivers and streams.

Longear sunfish and smallmouth and rock bass are mainly riverine, using rocky substrate. Uncommon northern longear sunfish are found in Lake Erie tributaries, especially the Auglaize and Grand Rivers while central longears are common in the Ohio River drainage. Rock bass inhabit deep holes in rivers and are common along Lake Erie's rocky shoreline. Smallmouth bass frequent deep holes with undercut banks and woody debris. Both were important to Lake Erie's early commercial fisheries. Historic accounts report large numbers of rock bass rising to the surface in spring to feed on swarms of emerging mayflies (Trautman 1981).

All of Ohio's centrarchids are nest-builders, with males vigorously defending nests and eggs. Males fan circular-shaped depressions in soft substrates using their caudal fins. Their nests vary in diameter, depending on species and size of the individual males. Nests fanned by basses can be three feet in diameter. Bluegill breed in large colonies in shallow water. After females lay their eggs, the males drive them from their nests and remain to fan and guard the eggs. Longear sunfish form small groups, choosing quiet pools and gravelly margins of riffles and runs. Pumpkinseed nests are more widely spaced, with preferred depths of less than four feet in aquatic vegetation. Warmouth sunfish typically place theirs near submerged stumps or tangles of vegetation.

Black and white crappies form loose nesting colonies in deeper water than other sunfish. White crappies have been observed at depths of eight to ten feet. In rivers, white crappies construct nests under overhanging banks, where their eggs are usually attached to rootlets. Largemouth bass typically place their nests in shallow water near shorelines. Rock bass are solitary spawners that often place their nests near logs or rocks. Before the construction of dams by European settlers in the nineteenth century large numbers of bass (both smallmouth and largemouth) migrated from Lake Erie into tributary streams to spawn. These newly constructed dams blocked many of the spawning runs and were a major contributor to the decline in Lake Erie bass populations. In the spring, prior to spawning, stream-dwelling smallmouth and spotted bass also make upstream migrations, which is followed by a downstream movement in late summer as water levels begin to drop. The construction of dams by Ohio's early settlers blocked many of these spawning runs as well.

Many centrarchids overpopulate their habitats, which results in stunted populations. A single bluegill can lay 38,000 eggs, and multiple females will lay eggs in the same nest. In one case, a single nest produced more than 60,000 young. Similarly, a pumpkinseed nest can produce as many as 14,000 young. Crappies are also prodigious egg layers; depending on its size, a female white crappie can lay anywhere from 10,000 to 160,000 eggs (Steiner 2000). Various species of sunfish are notorious for their ability to hybridize; green, bluegill, and longear hybrids are commonly encountered by biologists conducting fish surveys on Ohio streams. Hybrid bluegill and green sunfish are infertile and are widely sold to owners of ponds and lakes to control fish populations.

Centrarchids are primarily sight feeders, as evidenced by their large eyes. Crappies and bass, with their large mouths, prey heavily on minnows and other small fish. A top predator in the food chain, the largemouth bass will also take small snakes, frogs, and newly hatched waterfowl. Crayfish are a favored food item of smallmouth and rock bass. With strong jaws, stocky warmouth sunfish can take fish, crayfish, and other large prey. Pumpkinseeds eat thin-shelled snails, which they pluck from aquatic vegetation. Unlike other sunfish, they are primarily bottom-feeders. Smaller individuals have a more varied diet of terrestrial and aquatic insects. Sunfish and crappies sometimes form large schools, particularly in lakes and other impounded waters. The large populations of bass and sunfish described in the old canal lakes and the western basin of Lake Erie during the early years of the twentieth century are, regrettably, a thing of the past.

Rock bass inhabit dense rooted vegetation and rocky ledges in large streams as well as Lake Erie. Small crayfish make up a small portion of their diet. They can change color to fit their surroundings.

Bluegill are Ohio's most abundant sunfish. Adults may be stunted in overstocked ponds.

A stream species, the colorful central longear sunfish is restricted to the Ohio River drainage.

Ohio's smallest centrachids, orange-spotted sunfish are common in the Maumee River. This prairie stream species tolerates turbid water.

Largemouth bass fry school in Lake Erie; banding together gives young fish a better chance of survival.

Small populations of northern longear sunfish are found in the Grand and Maumee Rivers. They spawn in small communal groups.

White crappies are tolerant of turbid water. These sport fish are well distributed across the state and frequently stocked in lakes and reservoirs.

The green sunfish is one of Ohio's most abundant centrachids. It thrives in poor-quality water where there is little competition from other sunfish species, with which it frequently hybridizes.

Spotted bass inhabit streams in the Ohio River drainage; they are especially common in the Scioto and Muskingum Rivers.

Smallmouth bass fry have orange tail bars. Young feed on zooplankton and midge larvae.

Mainly a riverine species, the smallmouth bass is also common in Lake Erie around the islands of the western basin.

A southern species, the warmouth sunfish is local in Ohio. It can be found in the upper Cuyahoga River and many of the state's glacial lakes.

Common black crappie retire to deep water during hot summers. They are commonly stocked in many of Ohio's lakes and reservoirs.

Pumpkinseeds are named for the dark spots on their opercula. They are common in lakes and ponded streams, mainly in the northern half of the state.

Largemouth bass are common inhabitants of lakes and rivers, including Lake Erie. Popular sport fish, they are among the top predators in the food chain.

Darters
A Rainbow of Colors

CHAPTER 9

Darters are among the most colorful, fascinating, and highly complex group of North American freshwater fishes. They tend to be small, two to four inches in length. The source of their name is apparent to anyone who has ever waded in a clear stream and observed the various life forms fleeing at their approach. Darters do not swim away as other fish do but rather appear to dart along the stream's bottom in short bursts, often finding refuge under a rock or piece of woody debris. A careful look at a darter sitting on the stream bottom shows that darters sit up on extended pectoral fins. Depending on the time of year, the coloration (a combination of orange, red, blues, and greens) of some individuals might also be noticeable. Because of their active lifestyles and bright colors, darters are often justly referred to as the "butterflies of the fish world."

Darters belong to the Family Percidae, the same group that includes the more familiar yellow perch and walleye. A distinguishing feature of this family is the divided dorsal fin. The anterior fin is often spiny, unlike the soft-rayed posterior fin. Darters are, with few exceptions, a wholly North American group, occurring from Canada as far south as northern Mexico. They range from the eastern coastal plains west to the Continental Divide. Only one species, the Mexican darter, occurs west of this divide. Fossil evidence traces the origins of this group back to the Pleistocene Age, with the original center of distribution in the Mississippi Basin. Past ice ages have had a major impact on present distribution patterns as northern tributaries flowing into the basin were overrun or blocked by the advancing glaciers. These streams, including Ohio River tributaries in the glaciated portions of the state, date back to the last glacial event, about twelve thousand years ago. Fish found in streams unaffected by glaciation in the Mississippi drainage are far older, with more diversity. Today, the greatest number of darters are found within the Appalachian Highlands and the Interior Plateau regions of the eastern United States, especially in northern Alabama and eastern Tennessee. An abundance of darters is often a good indicator of stream quality. Some of Ohio's species—like bluebreast, variegate, banded, and spotted darters—are intolerant of disturbed habitats and pollution.

In recent years, taxonomic classification of darters based on observing morphological characteristics has given way to the use of comparative molecular and DNA studies. These types of data have allowed taxonomists to study the phylogenetic relationships among the various genera, species, and subspecies of darters. As a result, scientists are getting a clearer picture of their relationships. New species and subspecies have been and will continue to be described based on molecular studies.

There are currently more than 200 species plus numerous subspecies described, divided among four genera: *Etheostoma, Percina, Ammocrypta,* and *Crystallaria*. The *Etheostoma* is the largest genus, with more than 150 species. Its members are also the most colorful. The *Percina* comprises more than 45 named species and includes some of the largest darters. In Ohio, this distinction goes to the logperch darter, at around seven inches. Elsewhere, the freckled darter of the gulf states may reach nine inches. The *Ammocrypta* comprise six species of sand darter that are highly adapted to a life in the unsilted sandy substrates of larger rivers in which they burrow, leaving only their eyes exposed. They have little coloration and are mainly translucent. Their bodies are long, slender, and rounded, enabling them to dive into sand. Many populations are now greatly diminished, their sandy runs having been covered by silt. The genus *Crystallaria* comprises two species. One, the diamond darter, has only recently been described. The diamond darter is one of the continent's rarest fish, with only a single population known, this one in West Virginia's Elk River.

There have been twenty-two species of darters recorded in Ohio. One of these, the diamond darter, has not been collected in Ohio in more than one hundred years and is presumed extirpated. Until recently, gilt darters were known only from two pre-1900 collections; one in the Maumee River in Wood County and a second in the Ohio River in Gallia County. During surveys on the Ohio River in 2010, Brian Zimmerman and Justin Baker captured a single specimen of the gilt darter. Follow-up surveys on the Ohio in 2012 resulted in the capture of another five specimens of this rare darter (Zimmerman personal communication). A third species, the longhead darter, is known only from two collections made in the Walhonding River in 1939. It is presumed extirpated, as repeated attempts to collect it have been unsuccessful. Today the longhead is imperiled throughout its restricted range. With the reappearance of the gilt darter, twenty species are known to be extant in Ohio. Of this total, all twelve of the original representatives of *Etheostoma* can still be found, as can seven of the original eight species of *Percina*. Three of these twenty (Iowa, spotted, and gilt) are now listed as endangered, and another three (river, channel, and Tippecanoe) are listed as threatened.

Many darters are common statewide, but some are limited to tributary streams of the Ohio River Basin. The latter include banded, spotted, bluebreast, Tippecanoe, and variegate darters. Many of these populations are quite local, sometimes occurring on specific riffles. Iowa darters in Ohio occur at the southern edge of their range and are known primarily from a number of glacial lakes. Glacial lake studies in the 1980s found Iowa darters in eighteen of the lakes sampled (Phinney and Rice 1984). Unfortunately, recent surveys have documented the loss of many of these populations, and Iowa darters are now listed as endangered. Endangered spotted darters are most common in Big Darby Creek, where their population has recently expanded. Elsewhere in Ohio, they are known from a few riffles in the Walhonding and Kokosing Rivers. Originally found in both the Ohio and Lake Erie drainages, river and channel darters are listed as threatened. Recent trawl surveys in the Ohio River have revealed that river and channel darters are more common than previously thought. River darters have not been reported from the Lake Erie drainage in Ohio since the 1940s, and while there are more recent records of channel darters from the lake, the recent invasion of Lake Erie by the round goby threatens the current presence of these two darters here.

Darters are most often associated with riffles and runs in rivers and streams of all sizes. They possess adaptive traits that enable them to exploit these habitats. The majority of darters, with the exception of the Percina, essentially lack functioning swim bladders, which means riffle-dwelling darters can remain on the bottom without expending a lot of energy. Here among the gravel, cobbles, and boulders, darters carry out their daily activities. Other adaptive features present in some species—such as variegate, greenside, and river darters—include slightly flattened heads and large pectoral fins. Water flowing over their heads and bodies exerts a downward pressure, and the large pectoral fins act as stabilizers for maintaining position in strong current.

Riffles and runs offer several advantages as habitat niches for darters. Stronger current acts as a deterrent to potential predators and prevents the deposition of harmful silts on riffle substrates. Large rocks found on many riffles support a diverse community of aquatic macroinvertebrates, used as food. They also provide hiding, breeding, and resting places for many species. Riffles with fast current that have become compacted by silt deposition usually have few darters. Water temperature, current velocity, and substrate are the main factors determining whether darters are in riffles or pools. Darters may also be found in a variety of other aquatic habitats. A number of these, like the sand and channel darters, were once common in Lake Erie, where currents and wave actions on rock and unsilted sand mimic riverine habitats. Iowa and least darters are found in weedy, soft-bottomed streams and glacial lakes. Dusky darters are most often found in association with organic debris. Pollution-tolerant johnny darters, Ohio's most abundant species, inhabit sluggish pools; they can be found from the state's smallest streams to its largest rivers. A scaly form of this species inhabits Lake Erie.

Darters are known for their intense colors exhibited during the breeding season. Various patterns and colors have given rise to many species' common names. Rainbow, orange-throat, bluebreast, and greenside darters refer to the colors breeding males display. Red seems especially favored by females, because it is less visible to predators from a distance. While females may also show some coloration, they appear subdued in comparison to their flashy counterparts. The result is what biologists refer to as sexual dimorphism, common to many groups of animals. Sexual selection based on the color patterns of the males is thought one of the driving forces in the evolution of the Etheostoma genus, resulting in the high diversity of species we see today. A breeding male exhibiting color or pattern changes favored by a female will pass that trait on to the next generation. This ultimately may lead to a new population exhibiting traits that isolate it from neighboring populations, allowing for a new species to evolve. Good examples of this are the bluebreast and greenfin darter populations in the upper Tennessee River drainage of the Blue Ridge Mountains. Specification between these two very similar species has been based largely on differences in coloration. The intensity of colors displaying males exhibit may also enable rivals to size each other up in the competition for mates and defense of prime nesting territory. Many pool-dwelling species—like the johnny, least, blackside, and channel darter—have black and brown markings, which help them blend into sand and gravel substrates. The breeding male Iowa darter, a glacial relict species with brick-red bars, is an exception.

Darters employ a variety of reproductive strategies. A few species, like spotted and bluebreast, are cavity nesters. Males will prepare nest cavities under flattened rocks in suitable riffles or runs, then use their bright colors to attract females. The females lay a small number of relatively large eggs that adhere to the underside of the rock, after which the males will fertilize the eggs and guard them until they hatch. Johnny and fantail darters are cavity nesters that engage in cluster spawning; several females will mate and lay eggs in the same nest cavity, then males remain to guard the eggs. On the tips of their dorsal fins, breeding male fantail darters develop fleshy knobs that mimic eggs. Apparently, females prefer males that display these; they also seem attracted to males already guarding eggs from matings with other females. Other species also attach eggs to the undersides of woody debris or aquatic vegetation: Greenside darters attach theirs to strands of filamentous green algae on moss-covered rocks.

The females of many darter species simply lay their eggs over sand and gravel, where they are either buried or simply allowed to fall into interstitial spaces. This is true for many, if not most, of the *Percina* and *Ammocrypta* and many of the *Etheostoma*. For these, the mating ritual can be more involved. Males and females align themselves side by side, then rapidly vibrate their bodies, during which time eggs and milt are deposited. These movements also help bury the fertilized eggs. A study of spawning channel darters in Michigan found that males defended a territory of approximately one meter usually centered around a large rock. If a receptive female approached, the male would guide her into his nest. With the male resting on top of it, the female would partially bury itself in the gravel and then deposit its eggs (Winn 1953).

Darters are insectivorous, mainly feeding by sight. Their prey items include midge, caddisfly, stonefly, and mayfly larvae, and a variety of other aquatic macroinvertebrates. They may also eat algae and other forms of detritus. An analysis of the stomach contents of river darters collected in the Ohio River in Hamilton County revealed a diet composed almost entirely of midge larvae (Sanders and Yoder 1989). Another study showed a general similarity in feeding habits among the different species, particularly in the juvenile stage. The young preyed almost exclusively on entomostraca and small midge larva. Adults ate a variety of aquatic insect larvae, with lake darters having a more varied diet than stream species. Midge, mayfly, and caddisfly larvae composed most of the prey items of stream dwelling darters (Turner 1921).

Improvements in water quality in many Ohio streams since the late 1980s have resulted in the reestablishment of many uncommon species. Tippecanoe darters have increased throughout the lower Scioto River, and populations of bluebreast darter have expanded from the Walhonding River into the upper Muskingum. Since the 1990s, both species have moved into the upper Ohio River and its tributaries, such as Little Beaver Creek. Spotted darters, while still rare, have also increased in the Scioto drainage. Populations of eastern sand darters, once a candidate for federal listing, have also been expanding. Recent surveys have found populations throughout the Ohio drainage. Another notable expansion has occurred in the Maumee River. It is hoped that continued improvement in water quality will lead to further range expansions of this fascinating and beautiful family of fishes.

Spectacular variegate darters are restricted to Ohio River tributaries with fast currents and boulder-strewn riffles.

Tippecanoe darters are common in Big Darby Creek. This small darter is currently expanding its range into the Scioto and upper Ohio drainages.

A wide-ranging species, the blackside darter, like this male, can reach four inches in length.

Common banded darters are restricted to the Ohio River drainage. A series of vivid green bars identifies breeding males.

Cleaner streams have helped uncommon bluebreast darters expand their range in the Scioto, Muskingum, and upper Ohio drainages.

Dusky darters can be found in organic debris in southern Ohio rivers. Disjunct populations of this pool-dwelling species are also found in the Maumee Basin. Darters are important host fishes for freshwater mussels.

The knobs on this male fantail darter, which mimic eggs, are used to attract prospective females. Each male can mate with one or more females.

Ohio's largest darters, logperch are found under rocks in large rivers. Adults can grow to seven inches.

Iowa darters are found in weedy, soft-bottomed glacial lakes. Studies by George Phinney and Daniel Rice in the 1980s found populations in eighteen lakes. Surveys in 2012 and 2013 indicate the loss of some populations.

Gilt darters were absent from Ohio for over a century, but a few have recently been collected in the Ohio River.

A prairie stream species, the least darter is Ohio's smallest darter. These fish can be found in clean lakes and ponded streams.

Large populations of round gobies have probably eliminated scaly johnny darters from Lake Erie.

Greenside darters attach their eggs to strands of filamentous green algae. Common statewide, they can be found in large numbers in high-gradient riffles.

Rare throughout their limited range, longhead darters were last caught in the Walhonding River in 1939.

Slenderhead darters inhabit large rivers in southern Ohio. Elongated snouts and orange dorsal fin spots help identify this species.

Johnnies are Ohio's most abundant darter species. They inhabit streams of all sizes. When breeding, males' heads and fins darken.

Most abundant in Big Darby Creek, spotted darters are also local on a few riffles in the Walhonding and Kokosing Rivers.

Sand darters require clean, sandy runs in streams. Recent improvements in stream quality have helped Ohio populations expand.

Round gobies have probably eliminated threatened channel darters from Lake Erie. Populations of this deep-water darter are hard to quantify.

Threatened river darters inhabit deep water. Round gobies have likely eliminated most Lake Erie populations.

A prairie stream species, the spectacular orange-throat darter is found in the western half of the state.

Wide-ranging rainbow darters are one of Ohio's most colorful and abundant species. Favoring riffles and runs in the smaller streams, they begin spawning in April.

Fish of Lentic Habitats
Lake Erie

CHAPTER 10

A small number of Ohio's species are found only in Lake Erie. In the nineteenth and early twentieth centuries, several of these—burbot, cisco, and whitefish—were part of a thriving lake fishery. Still others—like walleye, muskellunge, northern pike, yellow perch, and white bass—are found in other lentic habitats in addition to Lake Erie. Today, many of these species are stocked throughout the state's lakes and reservoirs. Blue pike, a walleye subspecies, was formerly abundant in the deeper waters of the lake and contributed to a thriving commercial fishery. In the 1960s, the population experienced a total collapse from which it never recovered, and by 1970 it was considered extinct.

Sheephead, or freshwater drum, has one the widest distributions of any freshwater fish in North America extending from northern Canada south to Central America. It is the only member of its family to live its entire life in fresh water. Deep-bodied, the sheephead has a divided dorsal fin, a rather small rounded tail, and subterminal mouth. Most active at night, it moves into the shallows over sand and gravel substrates to feed on a variety of aquatic insect larvae, mollusks, and small crustaceans. Males emit grunting noises by vibrating specialized muscles against their swim bladders. When removed from water, they produce croaking sounds, which gives them common names like "grunt" or "croaker." During an extended spawning season, adults are believed to move into shallow water, where eggs and sperm are released. Fertilized eggs float to the surface, where current and wave action disperse them. Generally considered unpalatable for human consumption, large individuals can reach twenty pounds.

Burbot, related to cod, are the only freshwater member of this important group of marine fishes. Denizens of cold water, they are at the southern edge of their range in Lake Erie. Burbot frequent the central basin's deeper holes. This unique-looking species has been described as a cross between an eel and a catfish. Burbot's large mouths and long bodies are covered by small scales that exude copious amounts of slime. Their dorsal fins are divided, with the posterior fins elongated and extending to rounded tail fins. Elongated anal fins mirror the dorsal fins. Single barbels dangle from the chin, and one shorter tubelike barbel extends from each nostril. Their sides are mottled in dark brown and black. Burbot can be more than thirty-six inches long.

Active and voracious predators, they eat a variety of living prey. Burbot are one of the few fish that spawn in winter, moving into shallow water in late November. During spawning, males and females form large, quivering masses from which milt and eggs are released. Fertilized eggs drift along the bottom substrates, hatching in about thirty days. Eggs and young receive no parental care. Burbot populations declined in the Great Lakes during the middle of the twentieth century as a combination of over-fishing and the depredations of invading sea lampreys depressed commercial fish stocks. Populations have rebounded in recent years, with the initiation of a Great Lakes sea lamprey control program.

Today, the two most commercially important fish in Lake Erie are yellow perch and walleye. Both are in the Family Percidae, which also includes the darters. Walleye are its largest member in North America, attaining lengths of up to thirty-six inches. Their round bodies have divided dorsal fins composed of spinous and soft-rayed fins. Their coloration, although variable, is often gold with a series of dark saddles extending over the dorsal surfaces and pronounced black splotches at the posterior ends of the spinous dorsal fins. Their large mouths are filled with needle-sharp teeth, a fact to which more than one careless angler can attest.

Widely distributed across most of Canada and the eastern half of the United States, walleye have been introduced into areas outside their natural range. During the spring spawning season, sexually mature adults migrate into large tributary streams, where the females scatter eggs on rocky substrates. Construction of dams on many of these tributaries has blocked traditional spawning runs. Spawning walleye also use shallow reef areas in the western basin. Young walleye feed on a variety of zooplankton and aquatic invertebrates. Large individuals prey on a variety of fish, crustaceans, leeches, and macroinvertebrates. Primarily night feeders, they move into shallow water after dark, using their light-sensitive eyes to detect prey.

Once common in the Ohio River and some of its larger tributaries, walleye are now greatly outnumbered here by their close cousin, the sauger, which look similar to walleye but lack the dark blotch on the anterior end of the spinous dorsal fin. Additionally, the webbing between the sauger's spinous dorsal rays is marked by rows of round to oblique dusky spots. More tolerant of turbid water than walleye, sauger are smaller, reaching a maximum length of twenty-four inches. In the past, sauger were also abundant in Lake Erie, where they favored the shallow western basin. By 1968, the commercial catch had dwindled to a minuscule sixty-two pounds.

European settlers never considered yellow perch table fare; only after the decline of more desirable lake species like muskellunge, cisco, and whitefish did yellow perch become commercially important. A small, deep-bodied species seldom exceeding twelve inches, the yellow perch gets its name from its gold coloring. The yellow perch's sides are marked with a series of six to nine dark vertical bands. Like walleye and sauger, it has divided spinous and soft-rayed dorsal fins. The first two rays of its anal fins are also modified into sharp spines, useful as defensive weapons against unwary anglers. Unlike walleye and sauger, this fish lacks sharp conical teeth.

Yellow perch are found in Lake Erie's clear-water harbors and embayments of the western basin, where they often form large schools. These are usually segregated by size, with smaller fish inhabiting shallower water. They prefer areas of vegetation or submerged brush as spawning sites. Once laid, the eggs are covered by a clear gelatinous membrane and held together in a long thin strand; they float until becoming entangled in submerged vegetation. Perch eat a variety of aquatic insects, invertebrates, and the eggs and young of other fish and, in turn, are an important part of the diet of many species like northern pike, walleye, and bass.

Among Ohio fishes, northern pike and muskellunge are top predators in the food chain. They eat fish, small birds and mammals, frogs, and even snakes. Employing camouflage and stealth to ambush passing prey, these fish explode from a favored hiding place with a burst of speed that allows the luckless target little time to react. Similar in appearance, both have long torpedo-shaped bodies and duck-billed mouths filled with needle-sharp teeth. Small dorsal and anal fins sit far back on their bodies, juxtaposed to each other. They can be differentiated by their pigmentation patterns: the dorsal surfaces and sides of northern pike are olive-green with a series of yellow, barlike spots on the body and fins. Their cheeks are completely scaled. Muskellunge, however, have only the upper halves of their cheeks and gill covers scaled. Their body colors vary with age, water clarity, and habitat. The northern pike and muskellunge can both become quite large, with female muskellunge exceeding forty pounds.

Northern pike and muskellunge inhabit clear water with beds of aquatic vegetation and submerged logs. Prior to the construction of dams, they made spawning runs into Lake Erie tributaries. During the twentieth century, destruction of suitable habitat together with overfishing led to the total collapse of the lake's muskellunge population. These fish are particularly susceptible to overfishing, as their large sizes limit the number of individuals that can be sustained in a particular area. If they can survive their first few years, they are long-lived. Northern pike populations in Lake Erie also plummeted because of commercial fishing and loss of suitable habitat. Small numbers are still found in the western basin of Lake Erie and a few tributary streams, like the Maumee, Cuyahoga, and Portage Rivers.

Until the twentieth century, northern pike were limited to the Lake Erie drainage. Between 1952 and 1980, the Ohio Division of Wildlife stocked pike in a number of lakes and reservoirs in both Ohio River and Lake Erie drainages. In only a few instances did these stockings result in self-sustaining populations. Muskellunge are found statewide today; through the early years of the twentieth century, they were widespread and abundant in many of the Ohio River tributary streams, like the Muskingum and Scioto Rivers. Overfishing, pollution, and habitat destruction led to the same declines experienced in Lake Erie. Muskellunge were first raised at the Kinkaid Fish Hatchery in 1953. Subsequently, they have been stocked in a number of larger reservoirs and lakes, creating a successful sport fishery for this species. Natural self-sustaining populations are known today in only a few streams in southern Ohio.

Few fish could match the abundance of ciscoes in Lake Erie during the nineteenth century. Seldom exceeding fifteen inches in length, this small salmonid was harvested at a rate of 48 million pounds in 1916 alone (Trautman 1981). Ciscoes are identified by their slender bodies, silvery sides, and deeply forked tails. Schooling fish, they inhabit the deeper, colder waters of the central and eastern basin during most of the year. They spawn during the fall in shallow water, once temperatures drop to forty degrees. Their diet includes zooplankton, small crustaceans, and insect larvae. They are also important as forage for many larger predatory species, like lake trout. Despite their historical abundance, ciscoes were not highly esteemed as a food fish. In the pursuit of more desirable species, they were often discarded as a worthless byproduct. They did not become commercially important until the latter part of the nineteenth century, but by 1885 they were the most important commercial species in Lake Erie. In the first half of the twentieth century, their numbers began to fluctuate, and by the 1960s the population experienced a total collapse.

Lake whitefish, another Lake Erie salmonid, experienced a similar population decline. Deeper-bodied and larger than ciscoes, whitefish average eighteen inches in length. Unlike the cisco, they have small, subterminal mouths and rounded snouts. A schooling fish, it is found in deep waters of the central and eastern basins. Spawning begins in the fall, once water temperatures drop to fifty degrees. The females scatter eggs over rocky substrates, where they do not hatch until the following spring. Whitefish are bottom-feeders, using their small mouths to take a variety of crustaceans, insect larvae, and mollusks. Though not as abundant as ciscoes, they were much sought after for their mild taste. The commercial catch in Lake Erie mirrored that of the cisco, with the same fluctuations in the first half of the twentieth century, followed by an almost total collapse. Overfishing, pollution, and competition from introduced species contributed to the decline of both species. Improving habitat conditions in Lake Erie during the latter half of the twentieth century allowed for a modest increase in whitefish populations, which today support a small commercial fishery.

White bass belong to the Family Moronidae, or temperate basses. Their separated dorsal fins distinguish them from true basses, like the largemouth and spotted. Deep-bodied fish, they have smaller heads than true basses. They are silver-colored, with a series of fine horizontal stripes on their sides. Adults typically reach fourteen inches in length. They are schooling fish that frequent large rivers and lakes. Feeding by sight, they consume a variety of aquatic insects and small fish. They prefer riffles and runs in tributary streams as spawning areas, where the females scatter adhesive eggs over rocky substrates. Today, the Maumee and Sandusky Rivers are both noted for their spring runs of spawning white bass. During the early nineteenth century, white bass were so abundant that they dominated the commercial catch in the western basin of Lake Erie, and as with other commercially important species, a marked decline in population levels occurred by the middle of the twentieth century.

Abundant in Lake Erie, yellow perch are an important food fish. Quotas for commercial harvest are set every year based on the health of the current population.

The Maumee and Sandusky Rivers are noted for their spring spawning runs of white bass.

Sheephead, or freshwater drum, have the widest distribution of any North American freshwater fish.

Muskellunge are among the top predators in the food chain. Small populations are particularly susceptible to overfishing.

Northern pike were once stocked in many of Ohio's lakes and reservoirs. Ironically, zebra mussels helped clear Lake Erie water of algae and other suspended solids, causing northern pike to increase.

The largest member of the perch family in North America, walleye are Ohio's most important sport fish.

A small relative of the walleye, the sauger is especially common in the Ohio River.

Fish of Lentic Habitats 99

Aliens
Introduced Species

CHAPTER 11

Fish are constantly looking for new places to live. Alien species are deliberately or accidentally introduced into habitats far removed from their places of origin. These introductions can have disastrous consequences for native fish populations. Of all the nonnative fish found in Ohio, the European carp (also known as common carp), sea lamprey, and round goby have proven the most destructive. The European carp, a large member of the minnow family, was among the first species to be introduced. The releases began in 1879 and continued for another twenty years. Originally supplied to owners of ponds and small lakes, they soon escaped into surrounding streams. By 1890, they were found throughout the state. The turn of the twentieth century, however, saw carp as an important part of the commercial catch in Lake Erie, with smoked carp being a popular dish. As their numbers increased, they began to wreak havoc on aquatic environments, destroying aquatic vegetation through their rooting actions and causing irreparable damage to wetlands. Today, some lakes and reservoirs are almost devoid of vegetation, which greatly reduces numbers and abundance of other fish. Since the late 1980s, species like the bighead, silver, and grass carp have been imported and released in ponds to control algae and other types of unwanted vegetation. Not surprisingly, all have escaped from their enclosures. While the majority of the grass carp sold are sterile, bighead and silver carp are not and are spreading northward through the Mississippi Basin. These Asian carp pose a major threat to Great Lakes fisheries. They have already reached Chicago and are now poised to invade Lake Michigan, and it is possible they could also make their ruinous way north through

Ohio's tributary streams. If they gain access to Lake Erie, the consequences for sport fishing and tourism could be catastrophic.

Sea lampreys, as their name implies, are primarily anadromous, with adults living in marine environments then moving into freshwater to spawn. They occur on both sides of the Atlantic, primarily the eastern seaboard of the United States and the west coast of Europe. Niagara Falls was a major barrier preventing lampreys from moving into the Great Lakes until 1829, when the Welland Canal opened, allowing lampreys as well as ships access to the western Great Lakes. Colonization was slow, with the first sightings in Lake Erie occurring in 1921. Spawning individuals were observed in Swan Creek in Lucas County fifteen years later. Lake Erie populations remained small for a time, due in part to the poor habitat quality of tributaries required for spawning. Once firmly established, sea lampreys immediately started decimating trout and salmonid populations. Adult sea lampreys can reach twenty-five inches in length, and few fish are able to survive an attack by one of these parasites. To counteract lamprey infestations, the US Fish and Wildlife Service established a lamprey control group devoted entirely to reducing sea lamprey numbers in the Great Lake, primarily by using lampricides to kill ammocoetes in their spawning streams. In some streams, electrically charged barriers are used to block upstream movement. Cages are also employed to trap migrating adults. While the use of lampricides is highly destructive to lampreys, it also negatively affects some soft-bodied species, like mudpuppies and catfish.

Round gobies are one of the latest in a long line of unwanted species introduced into the Great Lakes from ballast water carried by ocean-going freighters. Gobies are bottom-dwellers, with large heads and powerful jaws. Adults are typically brown or grayish, with black markings. Originally native to the Black and Caspian Seas, round gobies were first discovered in the St. Clair River near Detroit in 1990. They rapidly spread, colonizing all of the Great Lakes. By 2002, the Ontario Ministry of Natural Resources estimated the population inhabiting the western basin of Lake Erie at approximately 10 billion individuals (Johnson et al. 2005). This shocking explosion in numbers can be explained by the species' high fecundity: females may spawn up to six times a year over a long breeding season, lasting from April to September. Multiple females may contribute to a single nest, which may contain up to five thousand eggs. Males aggressively defend the nest, eggs, and newly hatched young from all predators, resulting in successful hatching rates of 95 percent. The consequences for some of Ohio's native fish have been catastrophic. They have out-competed the resident sculpins and darters, driving some, like the scaly johnny darter, to the brink of extirpation. While gobies prefer mollusks, crustaceans, small fish, and aquatic macroinvertebrates, they will also eat fish eggs, putting pressure on bass and walleye populations. Unlike natives, they can feed at night, due to well-developed sensory receptors. While preferring rocky substrate, gobies are also able to survive in degraded conditions unsuitable for native fishes. Adult round gobies feed mainly on zebra and quagga mussels, giving some measure of control over these invasive species.

White perch, originally native to estuaries and freshwater systems along the Atlantic Coast, is another fish that gained access to Lake Erie via the Welland Canal. The first specimens were reported in 1953, but it wasn't until twenty years later that they started appearing in Ohio waters. White perch populations exploded during the 1980s, raising concerns about the fish's effect on sport fish populations. Young white perch consume the eggs and young of other fish, including walleye and white bass, while older individuals consume almost nothing but other fish. Another problem has been the appearance of white perch and white bass hybrids. Fertile hybrids are capable of back-crossing with either parent, producing hybrid swarms that could destroy white bass gene pools. Thankfully, white perch numbers began to level off in the 1990s; Lake Erie now supports a modest commercial harvest.

The alewife is another example of an Atlantic coast fish that gained access into Lake Erie through the Welland Canal. First reported in 1931, it reached its peak numbers in the 1960s, when many top predators in the lake were greatly diminished by overfishing and environmental degradation. Planktonic feeders, they formed large schools, competing with sport fish like yellow perch and white bass. Over the years, alewife numbers began to gradually diminish. Sensitive to temperature fluctuations, these fish are known for massive die-offs following inshore movements in spring. On the positive side, they have been an important food source for Great Lakes salmonid fisheries.

Rainbow smelt are another East Coast species to invade Ohio, in this case, as a result of escapes from Crystal Lake in Michigan. First reported in Lake Erie in 1932, they gradually increased in number. In spring, they move at night into shallow water to spawn, broadcasting eggs over sand and gravel. At this time, anglers would dip for them using large seines and nets. While they serve as an important prey item for many sport fish, they also have negative impacts. Adult smelt feed on the larva and young of many of these species, while their young compete with native fish for zooplankton and other macroinvertebrates. Smelt can reach lengths of ten inches and are commercially harvested in the Great Lakes. Lake Erie populations can fluctuate from year to year, with large spring die-offs occurring in some years.

Western mosquitofish are related to the killifish and topminnows. Small fish, they do not lay eggs but instead give birth to live young. With their stubby bodies, upturned mouths, and rounded fins, they resemble tadpoles. This southern species was first introduced into streams in the Oak Openings of Toledo in an effort to control swarms of mosquitos. Surprisingly, they can survive Ohio winters and persist locally in small numbers. During surveys at the Toledo Airport in the 1990s, mosquitofish were found to be thriving in shallow runway ditches. Recent surveys indicate small populations in many of the state's larger rivers in both the Ohio River and Lake Erie basins. Like other topminnows, they inhabit quiet pools of low-gradient streams. Aggressive by nature, they can out-compete native species for food. And they can quickly proliferate, with females producing between forty and a hundred young.

Thought the possible result of either aquarium releases or bait-bucket introductions, northern studfish were first reported in 1995, in Massie's Creek, a tributary of the Little Miami River. This species has currently expanded throughout the Little Miami system and is poised to invade other streams in southern Ohio. In 2012, according to Brian Zimmerman, a population was identified for the first time in the Sunfish Creek drainage in Pike County, where they are rapidly spreading throughout the system (personal communication). An introduced population in West Virginia has recently expanded across the Ohio River into some of the Belmont County tributary streams. Northern studfish are the largest and most colorful of the topminnows found in Ohio, reaching six inches in length.

A number of sport fish have been periodically introduced into Ohio waters since the 1870s in an effort to increase opportunities for fishermen. In most cases, these transplants failed to establish self-sustaining populations and were maintained only by continual stockings. Among the first species to be introduced in the 1880s were brown and rainbow trout. To survive, trout require water temperatures below sixty-five degrees. In the summers, most Ohio stream temperatures exceed that, which explains the failure of almost all efforts to establish viable populations. Only in a very few cold, clear, spring-fed streams, like Cold Creek in Erie County, did these fish reproduce naturally. Today both state and private conservation groups widely stock rainbow trout as a means of providing a put-and-take seasonal fishery.

Beginning in 1933, historically, chinook and coho salmon were periodically introduced into Lake Erie, with some of the largest releases occurring in the late 1960s and early 1970s. These efforts were largely unsuccessful. Stocking of these two species has been replaced by releasing steelhead trout into major tributaries in northeastern Ohio. Supported by continual stocking and successful reproduction, this program has provided a highly successful fishery for anglers. One of the few nonnative sport fish that has become successfully established is the redear sunfish. A southern species, it has been widely introduced into Ohio's lakes and reservoirs. Competition with other sunfish limits its numbers, and hybrids between redears and bluegill are frequent. Between 1954 and 1982, chain pickerel were introduced into some of the state's larger lakes. Evidence of natural reproduction was observed only in Long Lake in Summit County, where they were first introduced in 1935. No chain pickerel have been captured or stocked for many years, and this species no longer exists in Ohio.

Western mosquito fish were first introduced in Toledo's Oak Openings to help control insect swarms. A southern species, they can survive Ohio winters.

Common carp are Ohio's most destructive invasive fish. Their rooting actions destroy aquatic vegetation, upsetting ecosystems in lakes and streams.

Arriving in ballast water from Eastern Europe in the 1990s, round gobies immediately began to disrupt Great Lakes ecosystems. By 2002, more than 10 billion inhabited Lake Erie's western basin. Consequences for some of the state's native populations have been catastrophic, with the elimination of many small fish species.

Aliens 105

After white perch gained access to the Great Lakes, they began causing problems for walleye and white bass. Their numbers began to stabilize in the 1990s.

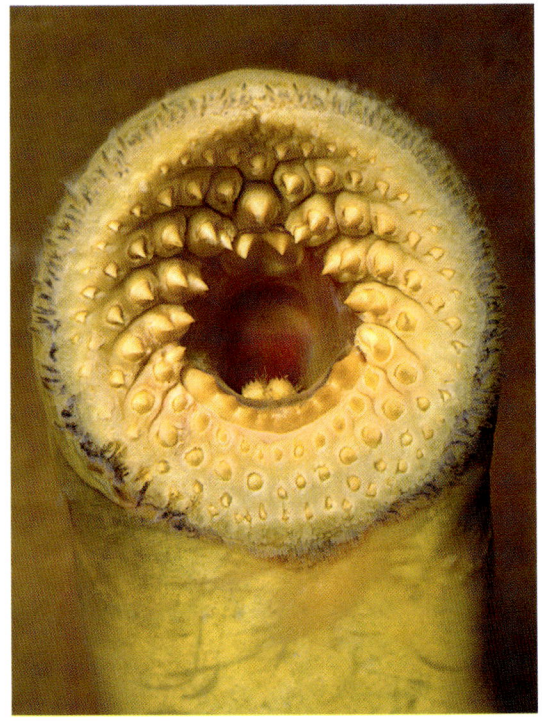

Sea lampreys invaded the western Great Lakes through the Welland Canal. These parasites have damaged lake trout and salmonid populations.

Glossary

adipose fin—a soft, fleshy fin found behind the dorsal fin of a fish.
aerate—to cause air to circulate.
algae—suspended plant organisms usually found in water.
ammocoetes—immature lampreys.
anadromous—migrating from saltwater to spawn in freshwater.
anal fin—the fin behind a fish's anus.
anterior fin—the first part of a divided dorsal fin.
benthic—the lowest level of a body of water (stream bottom).
cartilaginous—made of cartilage; calcified bone.
caudal fin—the tail fin of a fish.
crustaceans—a class of arthropods including shrimps, crayfish, crabs, and barnacles.
ctenoid scales—fish scales having comblike edges.
dorsal fins—the fins on top of a fish.
elver—a young freshwater eel.
endangered species—an imperiled species in a certain area.
endemism—a species restricted to a particular locality.
endomostraca—any of a large variety of crustaceans.
extinct—a species no longer in existence.
extirpated—exterminated in a certain area.
fecundity—the capacity of a female to produce young.
fry—a recently hatched fish.
genus—the main subdivision in a family of animals.

gill rakers—bony or cartilaginous projections in the gill, which function as filters.
hellgrammite—a large immature stage of the Dobson fly.
hybridization—two different species mating with each other and producing offspring.
lampricide—a chemical used to kill the larval and adult lampreys.
lateral line—part of a fish's acoustic hearing system, which runs down each side of its body.
lentic—still water, such as found in ponds and lakes.
intramuscular bones—muscle interlaced with calcified bone.
macroinvertebrates—small animals with no backbones.
madtom—a genus of small catfish.
marine—referring to saltwater.
milt—fish sperm.
morphology—the shape and structure of an animal.
notochord—a rod-shaped cord formed during embryological development in animals, replaced by the vertebral column in higher vertebrates.
opercle—the bony covering protecting the gills of a fish.
oxbow—a river bend that has become separated from a stream's main channel.
parasitic—living at the expense of another species.
pectoral fins—the paired fins just behind the head of a fish.

pheromones—chemical substances secreted externally by certain animals.

photoreceptors—rods and cones on the retina that receive light.

phylogenic—evolutionary descent of any plant or animal species.

phytoplankton—unicellular plants found suspended in aquatic habitats forming the base of the aquatic food chain.

posterior fin—the second part of a divided dorsal fin.

protrusible lips—fleshy lips on the underside of suckers and carp.

riffle—a shallow area in a stream usually at the head of a pool, characterized by rocky substrates and fast currents where there is a visible drop in elevation.

riparian—land directly next to a river or stream.

salmonid—referring to a species in the salmon family.

scute—an external bony plate found on fishes and reptiles.

seine—a large net used to capture fish.

spawn—to produce or deposit eggs.

taxonomy—the science of animal classification.

threatened—a species that is in decline.

translucent—diffused light that can pass through a fish's body.

tributary—water flowing into a larger stream.

turbidity—the clouding of water by suspended particulate matter.

vernal—referring to the spring.

xerothermic period—a warm dry glacial interval.

zooplankton—microscopic animals found suspended in aquatic systems.

Bibliography

Cooper, Edwin L. 1983. *Fishes of Pennsylvania and the Northeastern United States.* University Park: Pennsylvania State University Press.

Downhower, Jerry F. and Luther Brown. 1980. "Mate Preference of Female Mottled Sculpins '*Cottus bairdi.*'" *Animal Behavior* 28 (3): 728–34.

Hackney, P. A., W. M. Tatum, and S. L. Spencer. 1968. "Life History Study of the River Redhorse, *M. carinatum* (Cope) in the Cahaba River, AL, with Notes on Management of the Species as a Sport Fish." *Proceedings of the Southeastern Association of Game and Fish Commissioners* 21:324–32.

Hardisty, M. W. 1963. "Fecundity and Speciation in Lampreys." *Evolution* 17(1): 17–22.

Henshall, James A. 1888. "Contributions to the Ichthyology of Ohio." *Journal of the Cincinnati Society of Natural History* 11(1):76–80.

Henshall, James A. 1889. "Contributions to the Ichthyology of Ohio." *Journal of the Cincinnati Society of Natural History* 11(2):122–26.

Johnson, R. O. 1963. "Studies on the Life History and Ecology of the Big Mouth Buffalo *Ictiobus Cyprinellus* (Valenciennes)." *Journal of the Fisheries Research Board of Canada* 20(1):1397–429.

Johnson, Timothy B. et al. 2005. "Comparison of Methods Needed to Estimate Population Size of Round Gobies (*Neogobius melanostomus*) in Western Lake Erie." *Journal of Great Lakes Research* 31(1):78–86.

Kirsch, Phillip H. 1894. "A Report upon Investigations in the Maumee River Basin during the Summer of 1893." *Bulletin of the US Fish Commission* 14:315–37, table 1.

Kirtland, Jared P. 1838. "Report on the Zoology of Ohio." *Annual Report of the Geological Survey of the State of Ohio* 2:157–97.

———. 1851. "Piscatoriana. No. 5." *Boston Journal of Natural History* 2, No. 11:87.

Mayhew, J., ed. 1987. *Iowa Fish and Fishing.* Des Moines: Iowa Department of Natural Resources.

Morrow, James V. et al. 1998. "Age, Growth, and Mortality of Shovelnose Sturgeon in the Lower Mississippi River." *North American Journal of Fisheries Management* 18(3):725–30.

Osburn, Raymond C. 1901. "The Fishes of Ohio." *Ohio State Academy of Sciences, Special Paper* 4:1–105.

Osburn, Raymond C., Edward L. Wickliff, and Milton B. Trautman. 1930. "A Revised List of the Fishes of Ohio." *Ohio Journal of Science* 30(3):169–76.

Phinney, George J. and Daniel L. Rice. 1984. "Brief Note. New Records of the Iowa Darter, *Etheostoma Exile* (Percidae), in Ohio." *Ohio Journal of Science* 84(1):67–70.

Rafinesque, C. S. 1820. *Icthyolgia Ohiensis; or, Natural History of the Fishes Inhabiting the River and Its Tributary Streams, Preceded by a Physical Description of the Ohio and Its Branches.* Lexington, Ky.: W. G. Hunt.

Rice, Daniel, and George J. Phinney. 1985. "Distribution and Status of the Rosyside Dace, *Clinostomus funduloides* Girard (Cyprinidae) in Southern Ohio." *Ohio Journal of Science* 85(4):159–64.

Sanders, Randall E. et al. 1999. "The Frequency of Occurrence and Relative Abundance of Ohio Stream Fishes: 1979 through 1995." *Ohio Biological Survey Notes* 2:53–62.

Sanders, Randall E., and Chris O. Yoder. 1989. "Brief Note: Recent Collections and Food Items of River Darters, *Percina shumardi* (Percidae), in the Markland Dam Pool of the Ohio River." *Ohio Journal of Science* 89(1):33–35.

Steiner, Linda. 2000. *Pennsylvania Fishes*. Harrisburg: Pennsylvania Fish and Boat Commission.

Trautman, Milton B. 1957. *The Fishes of Ohio with Illustrated Keys*. Columbus: Ohio State University Press in collaboration with the Ohio Division of Wildlife and the Ohio State University Development Fund.

———. 1981. *The Fishes of Ohio with Illustrated Keys*. Revised edition. Columbus: Ohio State University Press in collaboration with Ohio Sea Grant Program and Center for Lake Erie Area Research.

Turner, Clarence L. 1921. "Food of the Common Ohio Darters." *Ohio Journal of Science* 22:41–62.

Winn, Howard E. 1953. "Breeding Habits of the Percid Fish *Hadropterus copelandi* in Michigan." *Copeia* 1:26–30.

Index

African lungfish, 10
alewife, 102
alligator gar, 9
Alosa, 7, 11–12, *15*
Ambloplites, 69, 70, 71, 72, 76
Ameiurus, 53, 54–55, *57, 59*
American brook lamprey, 2, 4
American eel, 12, *13*
Amiiformes, 10–11
ammocoetes, 2–3
Ammocrypta, 79, 81, 82, *90*
Anguillidae, 12
Asian carp, 100–101

Baker, Justin, 79
banded darter, 79, 80
banded sunfish, 69
bass, 69–72, *72, 74–77;* characteristics, 34, 69–72; habitat, 69–71, 92, 96, *97;* white perch/white bass hybrid, 102
bigeye chub (*Hybopsis*), 19–20, *25*
bigeye shiner, 32, 33, *39*
bighead carp, 100
bigmouth buffalofish (*Ictiobus*), 47–48
bigmouth shiner, 32, 33, 35, *39*
black bass (*Micropterus*), 69
black buffalofish (*Ictiobus*), 47
black bullhead catfish (*Ameiurus*), 54–55, *59*
blackchin shiner, 32, 34–35, *39*
black crappie (*Pomoxis*), 69, 70, 71, *77*
blacknose dace (*Rhinichthys*), 21, *23*
blacknose shiner, 32, *38*
black redhorse sucker (*Moxostoma*), 46
blackshin shiner, 33
blackside darter, 81, *84*
blackstripe topminnow (*Fundulus*), 62, *67*
bluebreast darter, 79, 80, 81, 82, 83, *85*
blue catfish (*Ictalurus*), 55
bluegill, 34, 70, 71, *73*
bluegill/green sunfish hybrid, 71
bluegill/redear hybrid, 104
blue pike, 92
blue sucker (*Cycleptus*), 45, 48
bluntnose minnow (*Pimephales*), 18, *26, 29*
bowfin, 7, 10–11, *14*

brindled madtom catfish (*Noturus*), 54, *58*
brook lamprey, 2
brook silverside, 60, 63, *67*
brook stickleback (*Culaea*), 60–61, *68*
brook trout, 60, 64, *65, 67*
brown bullhead catfish (*Ameiurus*), 54–55, *57*
brown trout, 103
buffalofish (*Ictiobus*), 45, 47–48
bullhead catfish (*Ameiurus*), 53, 54–55
bullhead minnow (*Pimephales*), 18, *27*
burbot, 92, 93

Campostoma, 18, *23, 24, 26*
carp, 100–101, *105*
Carpiodes, 45, 47, *51*
carpsucker (*Carpiodes*), 45, 47
Caspian sturgeon, 8
catfish, 53–56, *56–59;* characteristics, 53–56; habitat, 53–56; reproduction, 54
Catostomidae, 44–48, *49–52*
Catostomus, 44–45, 45, 46, 47, 48, *50*
central longear sunfish, 70, *73*
central mudminnow, 61, *66*
Centrarchidae, 69, 71–72
chain pickerel, 104
channel catfish (*Ictalurus*), 53, 55, *57, 58*
channel darter, 80, 81
channel shiner, 32, 34, *38*
chinook salmon, 103–4
chub, 19–20, 22, 24, 25, 28, 29, 30, 34
chubs, 16–22, *22–30;* characteristics of, 17, 19–20, 22, 24, 25, 28, 29, 30; *Erimystax,* 19; *Hybopsis,* 19; *Macrhybopsis,* 19, 20; *Nocomis,* 19, 20; *Semotilus,* 19, 20. See also Cyprinidae; *individual chub species names*
chubsucker (*Erimyzon*), 44–45, 46, 47, *51, 52*
cisco, 92, 94, 95–96
Clinostomus, 20–21, *22, 28*
Clupeidae, 11
coho salmon, 103–4
common banded darter, *85*
common black crappie, *77*

common carp (European carp), 100, *105*
common shiner, 33, 34, *37*
Cottidae, 63
crappie, 69–70, 71–72, *74, 77*
creek chub (*Semotilus*), 20, 22, *24, 28,* 34
creek chubsucker, 45, *51*
croaker (sheephead), 92
Crystallaria, 79
Culaea, 60–61, *68*
Cycleptus, 45, 48
Cyprinella, 31
Cyprinidae: minnow, chub, and dace, 16–22, *22–30;* shiner, 31–35, *35–43*

dace, 17, 20–22, *22, 27, 28.* See also Cyprinidae
darters, 78–83, *84–91;* characteristics, 78–83, 101–2; diet, 82; habitat, 78–81, 83; reproduction, 81–82; diamond darter (*Crystallaria*), 79; *Dorosoma,* 11, 12, *14;* drum (sheephead; grunt), 92, *98;* dusky darter, 81, *85*

eastern banded killifish (*Fundulus*), 62–63, *65*
eastern sand darter, 83
eastern shiner (*Notropis*), 31
eels, 12, *13, 14*
emerald shiner, 22, 32, 33, 34, *36*
Erimystax, 19, 20, *25, 30*
Erimyzon, 45, 47, *51*
Esocidae, 62
Etheostoma, 79–80, 81, 82, *87*
European carp (common carp), 100, *105*
European eel, 12
Exoglossum, 18, *30*

fantail darter, 82, *86*
fathead minnow (*Pimephales*), 18, *23*
fine-scaled shiner (*Lythrurus*), 31
flathead catfish (*Pylodictis*), 53, 56
fort-tailed catfish (*Ictalurus*), 53
freckled darter (*Percina*), 79
freshwater drum (sheephead; grunt), 92, *98*
Fundulae, 62
Fundulus, 60, 62–63, *65, 66, 67,* 103, *104*

111

gar, 7, 9–10, *15*
Gasterostsidae, 60–61
ghost shiner, 32, *43*
gilt darter (*Etheostoma*), 79–80, *87*
gizzard shad (*Dorosoma*), 11, 12, *14*
glass eel, 12
golden redhorse sucker (*Moxostoma*), 46, *49*
golden shiner (*Notemigonus*), 31, 33, 34, *41*
goldeye, 7, 11
grass carp, 100
grass pickerel (Esocidae family), 60, 62, *66*
gravel chub (*Erimystax*), 19, 20, *25*
greater redhorse sucker, 45
greenfin darter, 81
greenside darter, 80, 81, 82, *88*
green sunfish, 70, 71, *75*
green sunfish/bluegill hybrid, 71
grunt (sheephead; drum), 92, *98*

hagfish, 1
Hardisty, M. W., 2
harelip sucker (*Moxostoma*), 45
herring, 7, 11–12, *15*
highfin carpsucker (*Carpiodes*), 47
high-scaled shiner (*Luxilus*), 31
Hiodontidae, 7, 11
hogsucker (*Hypentelium*), 45, 46, *49*, *51*, *52*
hornyhead chub (*Nocomis*), 19, 20, *28*, *30*
Hybopsis, 25, 119–20
Hypentelium, 45, 46, *49*, *51*

Ictalurus, 53, 55, *57*, *58*
Icthyomyzon, 2
Ictobius, 45, 47–48
Iowa darter, 80, 81, *87*

johnny darter, 81, 82, *86*, *89*, 101–2

killifish (*Fundulus*), 60, 62–63, *66*, 103

lake chubsucker, 44–45, 46, *52*
lake darter, 82
Lake Erie, as habitat, 92–96, *97–99*
lake sturgeon, 8–9
lake trout, 95
lake whitefish, 96
Lampetra, 2
lamprey, 100, 101, *106*
lampreys, 1–4, *5–6*; characteristics of, 1–3, *6*; evolution and, 1; habitat, 3–4, 100, 101; *Icthyomyzon*, 2; *Lampetra*, 2; *Lethenteron*, 2; parasitic and nonparasitic lampreys, compared, 1, 3, *5*, *106*; *Petromyzon*, 2; reproduction, 2
largemouth bass (*Micropterus*), 34, 69, 70, 71, 72, *74*, *77*
least brook lamprey, 2, 4, *5*

least darter, 81, *87*
Lepomis, 34, 69–70, 71, 72, 77
Lethenteron, 2
logperch darter (*Percina*), 79, *86*
longear sunfish (*Lepomis*), 34, 69, 70, 71
longhead darter, 80, *88*
longnose dace (*Rhinichthys*), 21, *27*
longnose gar, 9–10, *15*
longnose sucker (*Catostomus*), 44–45, *45*
lungfish, 10
Luxilus, 31
Lythrurus, 31

Macrhybopsis, 19, 20
madtom catfish (*Noturus*), 53–54, *58*
May sucker (*Moxostoma*), 45
Mexican darter, 78
Micropterus, 34, 69, 70, 71, 72, 74, 75, *76*, *77*
mimic shiner, 33, 34, 35, *40*
minnows, 16–18, *23*, *24*, *26*, *27*, *29*, *30*. See also Cyprinidae
Minytrema, 45, 46, 47, *49*
mooneye, 7, 11
Moronidae, 96
mosquitofish (*Fundulus*), 103, *104*
mottled sculpin, 63, *68*
mountain brook lamprey, 2, 4, *6*
mountain madtom catfish (*Noturus*), 54, *58*
Moxostoma, 45, 46, 47, 48, *49*, *50*, *52*
mudminnow, 60, 61, *66*
muskellunge, 92, 94–95, *98*

Nocomis, 19, 20, *28*, *29*, *30*
northern brook lamprey, 2, 4, *6*
northern hog sucker, *52*
northern longear sunfish, 70, *74*
northern madtom catfish (*Noturus*), 54, *56*
northern pike, 92, 94–95, *99*
northern studfish (*Fundulus*), 103
Notemigonus, 31, 33, 34, *41*
Notropis, 31, 33, 35, *36*, *42*
Noturus, 53–54, *56*, *57*, *58*, *59*

Ohio lamprey, 2, 3, *5*, *6*
Opsopoeodus, 18, *26*
orange-spotted sunfish (*Lepomis*), 69, 70, *73*
orange-throat darter, 81, *91*

paddlefish, 7–8
perch, 60, 61–62, *65*, 92, 93, 94, *97*, 102, *106*
Percidae, 78, 93. See also darters
Percina, 79, 80, 82, *86*
Percopsidae, 64
Petromyzon, 2
Phenacobius, 24
Phoxinus, 20, 21, 22, *25*

pickerel, 60, 62, *66*, 104
pike, 92, 94–95, *99*
Pimephales, 18, *23*, *26*, *27*, *29*
pirate perch, 60, 61–62, *65*
Polyodontidae, 7–8
popeye shiner, 32, *37*
Poxomis, 69–70, 71, *74*, *77*
pugnose minnow (*Opsopoeodus*), 18, *26*
pugnose shiner, 31–32, 33, 34–35
pumpkinseed sunfish (*Lepomis*), 69–70, 71, 72, *77*
Pylodictis, 53, *56*

quillback carpsucker (*Carpiodes*), 47, *51*

rainbow darter, 81, *91*
rainbow smelt, 102–3
rainbow trout, 103
redear/bluegill hybrid, 104
redear sunfish, 104
redfin shiner, 33, 34, *36*
redside dace (*Clinostomus*), 20–21, *22*
Rhinichthys, 21, *23*, *27*
river carpsucker (*Carpiodes*), 47
river chub (*Nocomis*), 19, 20, *28*, *29*
river darter, 80, 82, *90*
river redhorse sucker (*Moxostoma*), 47
river shiner, 32
rock bass (*Ambloplites*), 69, 70, 71, 72, *76*
rosyface shiner, 33, 34, *43*
rosyside dace (*Clinostomus*), 21, *28*
round goby, 80, *86*, *90*, 100, 101–2, *105*

salmon, 103–4
salmonids, 95–96, 101
sand darter (*Ammocrypta*), 79, 81, *90*
sand shiner, 32, 33, 34, 35, *40*
satinfish shiner (*Cyprinella*), 31
sauger, 94, *99*
scaly johnny darter, *86*, 101–2
scarlet shiner, 32–33, 34, *37*
Scioto madtom catfish (*Noturus*), 54
sculpin, 60, 63–64, *68*, 101–2
sea lamprey, 2, 100, 101, *106*
Semotilus, 19, 20, 22, *24*, *28*, 34
shad, 7, 11–12
sheephead (freshwater drum; grunt), 92, *98*
shiners, 16, 31–35, *35–43*
shoal chub (*Macrhybopsis*), 19, 20
shorthead redhorse sucker (*Moxostoma*), 46, 47, 48, *52*
shortnose gar, 9, 10
shovelnose sturgeon, 8
silver carp, 100
silver chub (*Macrhybopsis*), 19, 20
silverjaw minnow (*Notropis*), 33, 35, *36*, *42*
silver lamprey, 2, 3–4
silver redhorse sucker (*Moxostoma*), 46, 47, *50*

silver shiner, 33, *41*
silverside, 60, 63, *67*
skipjack herring (*Alosa*), 7, 11–12, *15*
slenderhead darter, *89*
smallmouth bass (*Micropterus*), 69, 70, 71, *72*, 76
smallmouth buffalofish (*Ictobius*), 47
smallmouth redhorse sucker (*Moxostoma*), 46, *50*
smelt, 102–3
southern mosquitofish (*Fundulus*), 103
southern redbelly dace (*Phoxinus*), 20, 22, *25*
spoonhead sculpin, 63–64
spotfin shiner, 33, 34, *38*
spottail shiner, 32, 33, *42*
spotted bass (*Micropterus*), 69, 70, 71, *75*
spotted darter, 79, 80, 82, 83, *89*
spotted gar, 9, *10*
spotted sucker (*Minytrema*), 45, 46, 47, *49*
steelcolor shiner, 33, 34, *35*
steelhead trout, 104

stickleback, 60–61, *68*
stonecat madtom catfish (*Noturus*), 54, *59*
stoneroller minnow (rot-gut minnow) (*Campostoma*), 18, *23, 24, 26*
streamline chub (*Erimystax*), 19, 20, *30*
striped shiner (*Luxilus*), 31, 33, 34, *36, 41, 42*
studfish (*Fundulus*), 103
sturgeon, 7–9
suckermouth minnow (*Phenacobius*), 24
suckers (Catostomidae family), 44–48, *49–52*; characteristics, 44–48; habitat, 45–47; reproduction, 47
sunfish, 34, 69–70, 71, 72, *73, 74, 75, 76, 77,* 104

tadpole madtom catfish (*Noturus*), 54, *57*
threadfin shad, 11–12
Tippecanoe darter, 80, 83, *84*
tongue-tied minnow (*Exoglossum*), 18, *30*
topminnow (*Fundulus*), 60, 62, *67*, 103
trout, 60, 64, *65, 67,* 95, *101,* 103, 104
trout-perch, 60, 64, *68*

variegate darter, 79, 80, *84*

walleye, 92, 93–94, *99,* 102
warmouth sunfish, 69–70, 71, 72, *76*
western banded killifish (*Fundulus*), 62, 63, *66*
western mosquitofish (*Fundulus*), 103, *104*
white bass, 92, 96, *97*
white crappie (*Pomoxis*), 69–70, 71, *74*
whitefish, 92, 94
white perch, 102, *106*
white perch/white bass hybrid, 102
white sucker (*Catostomus*), 43–44, 45, 46, 47, 48, *50*

yellow bullhead catfish (*Ameiurus*), 54–55, *59*
yellow eel, 12
yellow perch, 92, 93, 94, *97*

Zimmerman, Brian, 3–4, 19, 61, 79–80, 103